STRIP PATCHWORK

QUICK AND EASY PATCHWORK
USING THE SEMINOLE TECHNIQUE

TAIMI DUDLEY

VNR VAN NOSTRAND REINHOLD COMPANY
New York Cincinnati Toronto London Melbourne

Printed in the United States of America
Designed by Loudan Enterprises

Published by Van Nostrand Reinhold Company
A division of Litton Educational Publishing, Inc.
135 West 50th Street, New York, NY 10020, U.S.A.

Van Nostrand Reinhold Limited
1410 Birchmount Road
Scarborough, Ontario MIP 2E7, Canada

Van Nostrand Reinhold Australia Pty. Ltd.
17 Queen Street
Mitcham, Victoria 3132, Australia

Van Nostrand Reinhold Company Limited
Molly Millars Lane
Wokingham, Berkshire, England

16 15 14 13 12 11 10 9 8 7 6 5 4 3 2 1

Library of Congress Cataloging in Publication Data

Dudley, Taimi.
    Strip patchwork.

    Bibliography: p.
    Includes index.
    1. Patchwork—Patterns.   2. Needlework—Patterns.
3. Indians of North America—Florida—Textile industry
and fabrics.   4. Seminole Indians—Social life and
customs.   I.   Title.
TT835.D86   746.46   79-25340
ISBN 0-442-20400-0

Front jacket photograph: Colors and patterns found in African textiles are reinterpreted here in strip patchwork. The wall hanging, which was made to simulate a Peruvian woven rug, and the pillows were made of woolen fabrics, rather than the firmly woven cottons used by the Seminoles. Pillows and hanging designed by the author. Pillows made by the author; hanging made by Adele Byrd.

Back jacket photograph: The long, narrow hanging borrows its color theme and its bold, simple pattern-bands from the typical dress of Seminole men of the 1890s. Strips of varying widths of plain colors were beautifully arranged in the intervening spaces to give rhythm and unity to the design. The apron on the back of the chair is an authentic Seminole apron with typical pattern-bands edged with narrow strips of contrasting colors. It is further embellished with narrow strips of appliqué. Similar patterns were used in the pillow but have a very different effect when carried out in only two colors, demonstrating the versatility of the strip technique. Hanging designed and made by Kay Kelly. Pillow by the author.

DEDICATION

To the memory of my mother, Emma Nelson, who was a superb seamstress and an excellent teacher. Although she was a perfectionist with regard to her own handiwork, she managed never to discourage her daughters' early attempts at sewing and embroidery, and conveyed to us a deep appreciation of elegance in workmanship and materials.

ACKNOWLEDGMENTS

At the top of my list of thank you's must come the name of my long-time friend, Mary Hanson, the instigator of this project, who shares with me an abiding passion for patterns, and whose wide-ranging knowledge of the textile arts has been my first and best resource. Loving thanks are due also to one Bill Dudley, who has supported my efforts with pride and affection, and who has performed a hundred small, helpful tasks.

For the splendid photography, which is so important to a work of this kind, I am deeply indebted to Harold Tacker. The fine pen-and-ink drawings were done by Kathie Dudley, my friend and daughter-in-law, whose understanding of sewing, as well as of graphic art, was of immeasurable help in a difficult and demanding task.

To the many persons who generously contributed examples of their work for the photography, I tender my sincere appreciation. Their names are mentioned where their works appear. I also wish to thank Sylvia and Harold Tacker and Jean Wilson for their friendly interest and many helpful suggestions.

CONTENTS

PREFACE

My interest in strip patchwork goes back several years. Curiously enough, for some time I had been using my own version of the strip patchwork technique without realizing it. It all started many years ago with a one-page article in *McCall's* that I had seen, yet virtually forgotten. It must have made quite an impression on me subconsciously, however, because I began to formulate my own strip patchwork technique. It wasn't until years later, when someone mentioned Seminole patchwork to me that I made the connection.

Urged to explore the subject by the members of my stitchery group, I went blithely to the library expecting to find at least one or two books on the subject. I could hardly believe that not even one existed.

From my original intention to provide a few photocopied sheets of my own devising, or to put together a small pamphlet, has grown the present book. The basic idea of sewing fabric strips together, cutting the resulting bands apart, and reassembling them in various ways seems so simple and obvious that I still wonder why its inherent possibilities have not been more extensively explored by someone before me. Perhaps my respect and affection for the sewing machine, plus my delight in patterned surfaces of all kinds, make me peculiarly suited to this task. Naturally, I hope many others who enjoy machine sewing will find this book useful and stimulating.

INTRODUCTION

Strip patchwork is a unique American folk art that makes use of the products of modern technology—the sewing machine, factory-woven cotton cloth, and scissors—to make beautifully patterned fabrics. In this unusual system, created by the Seminole Indians of Florida, strips of material in various colors are sewn together to form striped bands. These are then cut into segments, rearranged, and sewn together again to form the distinctive pattern-bands that are an integral part of Seminole garments.

This interesting and practical technique lends itself to endless creative experimentation. By changing the type of fabric used, the colors selected, the size and scale of the strips sewn together, a wide variety of effects can be achieved, ranging in style from the ethnic to the contemporary. "African" pillows, a "Navajo" blanket, traditional quilt blocks, bands and borders of all kinds, stunning contemporary graphics, even pictorial and floral motifs can be created by combining elements cut from machine-sewn bands of fabric.

Although not as complicated as it appears to be, strip patchwork does require the same care and accuracy in marking and cutting as does ordinary patchwork or good dressmaking. However, speed and precision are built into the system by the use of the sewing machine and the long parallel strips. The many seams intersecting one another produce a sturdy and attractive surface texture. The result is a quilted look without the time-consuming labor of hand-quilting.

Strip patchwork is an especially effective medium for studying the functions of color and value in determining pattern. Experimentation with these factors can lead to exciting new perceptions and can result in the discovery of a fascinating world of seemingly limitless patterns.

The first chapter gives detailed step-by-step directions for the basic technique, discusses suitable fabrics and their treatment, and lists the equipment needed. Chapter 2 contains examples of typical Seminole pattern-bands as seen in skirts and aprons, and gives specific directions for making them. In addition to showing examples of variations on Seminole patterns, Chapter 3 discusses the role of color in the structure of design, suggests experiments with colors and values in building effective patterns, and gives detailed information on how to design one's own original patterns and how to calculate the dimensions of the strips and the total amount of fabric needed for your original projects.

Ensuing chapters are devoted to the strip-sewing technique for quilt making, for clothing, and for making woolen pillows and other articles of home decoration. Complete step-by-step directions for several specific articles are included in each category. For the person who makes bags, pillows, aprons, or other small articles to be sold in gift shops or bazaars, strip patchwork has some very special advantages, and these are dealt with in the chapter on boutique sewing. The final chapter gives complete directions for constructing a beautiful Christmas banner, which can be varied or simplified to suit the taste or the ability of the maker.

It is my hope that others will find strip patchwork as practical, as logical, and as fascinating as I do.

C-1. The arresting pattern in this wall hanging, designed and made by the author, was done with pieces cut from a single strip-band of six colors, sorted and arranged to make the dark and light octagons. It is only one example of the immense variety of patterns that can be made with the strip technique. (See Figure 4-4.) In the yellow pillow, designed and made by Pat Albiston, sewn strips were cleverly used to make the trim for the corners, with tassels added. (See Figure 7-11.) The second pillow, made by the author, is an interpretation of the traditional Log Cabin quilt pattern known as Courthouse Steps. The lovable pink salamander, designed and made by Phyllis Bradfield, was also made of machine-sewn strips.

C-2. Typical Seminole patterns are given a contemporary feeling in this lovely set of place mats made by Rosemary King. (See Figure 7-13.) On the wall is a charming baby quilt made by Barbara Rickey in the Nine Patch pattern. The small box in the foreground (see Figure 7-14) is by Pat Albiston.

C-3. The narrow strips that form the fabric for this vest provide it with the warmth, as well as the appearance of quilting, and make a garment that is durable as well as attractive and wearable. Designed and made by the author. In the handsome caftan, presewn striped fabrics were made for the front panel. The speckled areas were formed by cutting and resewing narrow "slices" of the sewn stripes to make a pleasant random design. Horizontal bands and patterned areas were spaced to flatter the wearer. Designed and made by Donna Prichard.

C-4. This attractive skirt is truly quick and easy to make, requiring hardly any more time than it would to sew up two lengths of fabric to make a straight dirndl skirt. To make one like it see Figure 6-24. Designed and made by the author.

C-5. Typical Seminole patterns are well-suited to the design of the Christmas tree in this holiday banner. Banner designed and made by the author. (See Figure 8-1.) The pine branches are decorated with tiny Seminole dolls such as those seen in Figure 2-15, and a similar one made by the author. The stuffed dolls are also made by the author, and the small pillows were made by Lassie Wittman.

C-6. In the green vest shown vertical bands of diagonal stripes were inserted down the front and form an interesting yoke in the back. Vest designed and made by Phyllis Bradfield. The long inch-wide segments that compose the fabric in the brief bolero shown make a pattern of diagonal squares along the front edge. In the back the same small squares appear vertically to create a different pattern. The design was planned and carried out by Donna Prichard to demonstrate an idea by the author.

C-7. The immense versatility of the strip technique is demonstrated in this group of articles. The small coverlet on the wall is made of diagonal half-squares cut from a variety of bands, each band of three strips. The bands were joined in a pleasing, random design. (See Figure 4-3.) Coverlet by Liz McCord. The pattern in the large bag hanging from the chest was also made of diagonal half-squares cut from sewn bands. (See Figure 7-3.) The one on top of the chest uses a simple pattern very effectively. Both bags designed and made by Lassie Wittman. On the chest is a small box made by Pat Albiston and a linen bag by the author. (See Figure 7-1.) Corduroy, velveteen, and woven braid were used by Liz McCord to make the handsome, though simple, pillow on the floor.

C-8. This beautiful wall quilt, with its "painterly" use of color and interesting selection of patterns, demonstrates the scope of the strip technique as a medium for individual expression. Designed and made by Phyllis Bradfield. On the chair is a wool pillow based on a traditional quilt pattern, made by the author. (See Figure 4-38.)

C-1

C-2

C-3

C-4

C-5

C-6

C-7

C-8

A BRIEF HISTORY

When the first settlers arrived in the New World, there were no Seminole Indians. The people who bear this name today are descendants of the Creek Confederacy of Tribes. These people occupied some of the best farmlands in Georgia and Alabama and lived on good terms with the English from the earliest days of colonization, adapting themselves easily to many of the English customs and institutions. Then in the early 1700s they were pressured by the settlers to move into Florida, which was then owned by Spain. It was at about this time that they began to be known as the Seminoles, which in the Creek language means "wild people."

Florida was ceded to England by Spain in 1763 and then returned to Spain by treaty in 1783. The Seminoles continued to live in peace and prosperity under Spanish rule. They owned farms and citrus groves, large herds of cattle and horses, and kept black slaves, many of whom were runaways from white owners. Around 1814, the border skirmishes between Indians and white settlers, plus the fact that the Indians had been harboring slaves, gave the United States an excuse to invade Florida, and in 1819 Florida was purchased by the United States.

The Seminole lands were coveted by the white settlers; the Treaty of Moultrie Creek, signed in September 1823, forced the Seminoles again to move south. Hardly ten years later, the Florida settlers and the United States government were insisting upon removal of all the Indians to Indian Territory in Oklahoma. Although some of the peace-loving Indians were in favor of moving west, the majority of the tribe, inspired by the young Creek leader Osceola, refused. After prolonged efforts to settle these matters proved fruitless, the United States entered into the longest, costliest, and most difficult Indian war in its history. For nearly seven years the Seminoles fought a war of evasion. When the war was ended by agreement in 1842, three hundred and sixty survivors hid in the wilderness, never having signed a peace treaty with their conquerors.

After another "small" war, which broke out in 1855 and lasted for two years, reparations were finally paid to Chief Billy Bowlegs, the last Seminole leader left in Florida. He moved west with one hundred and thirty-nine people, leaving behind only one hundred and fifty, who disappeared into the Everglades. The Seminoles we know today are the descendants of the proud and unyielding remnant that stayed in Florida. Much of their history from that time until the beginning of this century remains unknown to us.

In 1891 the first land was set aside by the United States government for Seminole use, and, since then, other lands have been set aside or reserved for them in trust. Incredible as it may seem, however, Seminole children were not admitted to the public schools of Florida until 1946, although an Act of Congress in 1924 did declare the Seminoles to be citizens of the United States.

While assimilating more and more into the prevailing culture, the Seminoles today carefully preserve the best of their own. It is an irony that these people, who, from the beginning, showed a strong inclination to adapt to the ways of the newcomers to their land, were driven to retreat to a more primitive way of life than they might have chosen.

1

THE PRINCIPLES OF STRIP PATCHWORK

To acquaint you with the fundamentals of the Seminole technique I recommend that you make two or three of the sample pattern-bands given in this chapter. Should you choose to skip the actual construction of the samples, be sure to familiarize yourself with the material, as it includes the general directions for making all pattern-bands, lists the equipment needed, defines the terms used, and makes recommendations concerning fabrics.

EQUIPMENT

Basically, the following materials are all you need:
Sewing machine
Iron and ironing board
Scissors
Thread
Straight pins
Pens and/or pencils (washable or waterproof)
Triangle
Yardstick
Ruler

A transparent ruler, or a 2-inch-wide graph-marked ruler is a great convenience. Also, a bamboo point-turner, a large yarn needle, or a similar tool is helpful for holding the segments firmly in place as you sew.

FABRICS

It is best to use fabrics that can be torn readily. An examination of the garments made by the Seminole women reveals that the strips composing the pattern-bands are torn, not cut. Not only is tearing much quicker than cutting, but it assures parallel edges, which are essential for accurate matching of segments. To tear the fabric easily cut in from the selvage about 2 inches to get a good start. Of course, if you happen to have lengthwise scraps of material on hand, they may be used. Some fabrics can be torn lengthwise, but, if not, mark and carefully cut.

It is important to use the same weight of material in any one article to avoid problems in sewing. Suitable fabrics are firm, medium-weight cottons and cotton blends, such as percale, broadcloth, and gingham; sports weight materials, such as sailcloth, denim, corduroy and velveteen; and firm silks or synthetics, such as taffeta, satin, or brocade. Woolens of the approximate weight of flannel or gabardine may also be used. In fact, discarded woolen garments provide a good, economical source of fabric for many attractive projects.

It is considered good practice to prewash all fabrics. This means putting the fabric in the washer with detergent and running it through the cycle. Obviously, any article intended to be washable should be preshrunk. It is also important to remove the finishes with which most fabrics are treated, as these often cause problems in sewing, dull the needle rapidly, and create abrasive particles that can clog the machine. Furthermore, these particles will be contained in the dust that occurs when tearing the strips and could be harmful to breathe.

Colors used in authentic Seminole patchwork are bright and extremely varied. Strongly contrasting colors and values are essential to the effectiveness of the patterns. Most often, solid colors are used, but patterned fabrics may be employed, sometimes to great advantage in the design.

For constructing the sample pattern-bands, I suggest that you use plain, firmly woven medium-weight cotton in two colors—one light and one dark in value. For a quieter effect, two shades of one color or of related colors could be used. The use of color is perhaps the most crucial element in determining the effect of the pattern. There will be more about color and pattern in Chapter 3.

TERMS

The following terms are used repeatedly throughout the book, so it is a good idea to become familiar with their meanings.

Strip
Fabric measured and torn off crosswise to be sewn to another piece.

Strip-band
Two or more **strips** sewn together to be cut into **segments.**

Segment
A narrow piece cut from a **strip-band,** vertically or diagonally.

Pattern
The distinctive geometric design formed by sewing **segments** together.

Pattern-band
The completed decorative band or border formed by sewing **segments** together in an orderly repetitive system.

Patch
A combination of two or more differing **segments** sewn together to form a **motif** or **pattern.**

Motif
A figure used repeatedly in a design.

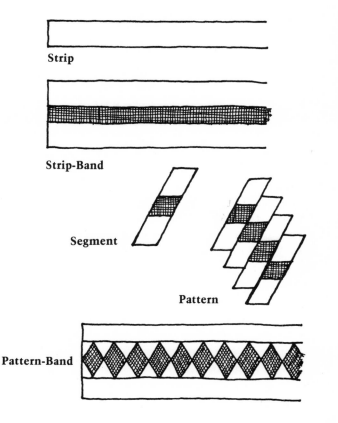

Strip

Strip-Band

Segment

Pattern

Pattern-Band

Patch

Motif

11

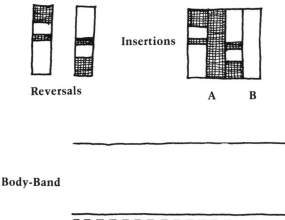

Insertions

Reversals

A   B

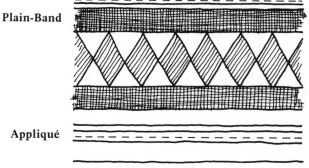

Body-Band

Plain-Band

Appliqué

Reversals
Segments from the same band turned about so that the colors alternately face in opposite directions.

Insertions
Segments of a single color sewn between multicolored segments to create a **motif** or to segregate **motifs** in a series.

Body-band
One plain-color fabric sewn repeatedly between **pattern-bands** to form the background or body of a garment.

Plain-band
A single-color band sewn between a **pattern-band** and a **body-band.**

Appliqué
Narrow strip of cloth, bias tape, rickrack, or combinations of all of these, sewn to the surface of the **body-bands** and/or **plain-bands.**

GENERAL DIRECTIONS FOR PATTERN-BANDS

Although strip patchwork is relatively simple in concept and execution, care and precision are required in preparing the strip-bands and in marking and cutting the segments.

1. Use two colors in plain 45-inch-wide fabric, one light and one dark for contrast. Before measuring off the width of the strip to be used, to assure a straight edge tear a narrow strip from the end of the fabric.

2. Mark a 3½-inch strip on each color, clip in from selvage about 2 inches for ease in tearing, and tear off strips. Press to remove puckering from edges.

3. Set the stitch length on your sewing machine to about 10 per inch. This is a fairly long stitch and will make it easier to rip out any mistakes made on your first samples. Sew the two strips together, taking a ¼-inch seam.

4. Press seam allowance toward the darker color, keeping the band straight as you press it.

5. With this sewn band still on the ironing board, wrong side up and dark color at the bottom, pin so that the seam is straight. Use a long straightedge and a few pins, as shown in Figure 1–1.

For the first three pattern samples given here use segments 1½ inch wide. (After seams have been sewn, you will end up with 1-inch-wide segments.) Since the fabric used is 45 inches wide, it will yield thirty segments, which divides conveniently into ten segments for each sample. To begin marking the cutting lines for the segments use a triangle or square to draw a vertical line at one end, as shown in Figure 1–2.

Mark at 1½-inch intervals from this line along the top and bottom of the strip-band, and draw lines joining these marks. Check to see that the fabric is straight, and cut all thirty segments.

The transparent graphed ruler can be used to establish the vertical and also to mark the cutting lines, by placing it as shown in Figure 1–3. Continue in the same manner across the band. A transparent dressmaker's ruler could be similarly used, or a cardboard pattern the width of the segment could be made.

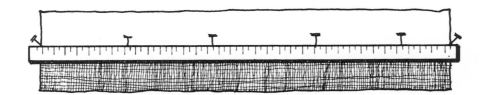

1-1. Straighten the seam in the strip-band by using a yardstick and pins.

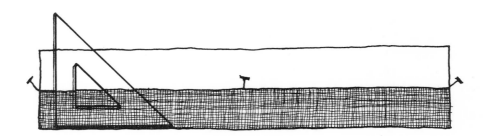

1-2. Use a triangle or square to ensure that the end of the band is square.

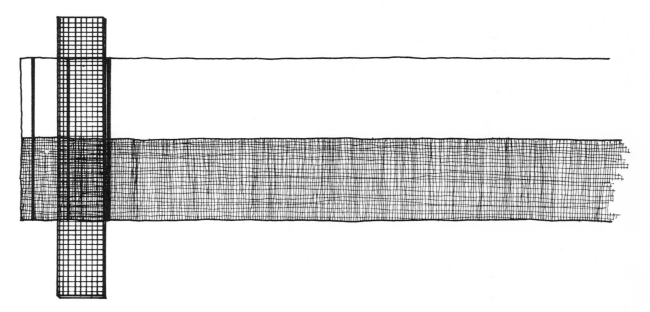

1-3. A transparent graphed ruler is convenient for marking segments.

PATTERN #1

To make the first pattern (see Figure 1–4), take ten of the segments and set the rest aside.

1. Lay ten segments in a row on the sewing machine, to the left of the presser foot, reversing alternate segments to form a checkered pattern. Mentally, number them one to ten from right to left. Do not actually mark the segments, but lay them in the order shown in Figure 1–5, right side up.

2. Following this order, turn Segment # 1 over onto Segment # 2, match the seams with a pin, and sew a ¼-inch seam along the right-hand edge of the segments, as in Figure 1–6a. Seams must match exactly. With the wrong side of the fabric up, finger-press the seam toward the left, as shown in Figure 1–6b.

3. Take Segment # 3, keeping it right side up, and place the two sewn-together segments over it, wrong side up, as in Figure 1–6c. Match seams, pin, sew, and finger-press as before (see Figure 1–6d). Continue sewing and finger-pressing until all ten segments are joined, keeping the completed work on top.

   Note: When pinning, the segment being added to the row always goes on the bottom.

4. Press the completed pattern-band lightly on the back so that all the seams lie in one direction.

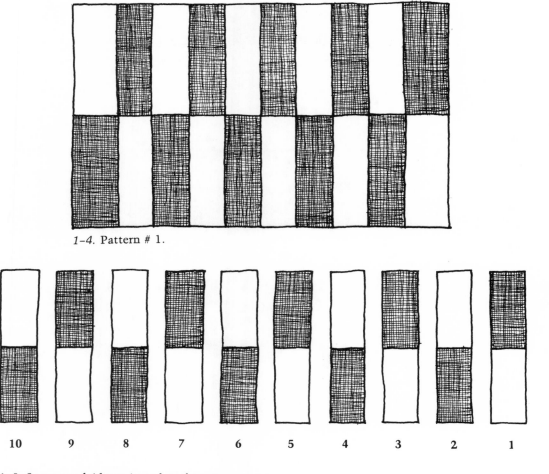

1–4. Pattern # 1.

| 10 | 9 | 8 | 7 | 6 | 5 | 4 | 3 | 2 | 1 |

1–5. Segments laid out in order of sewing.

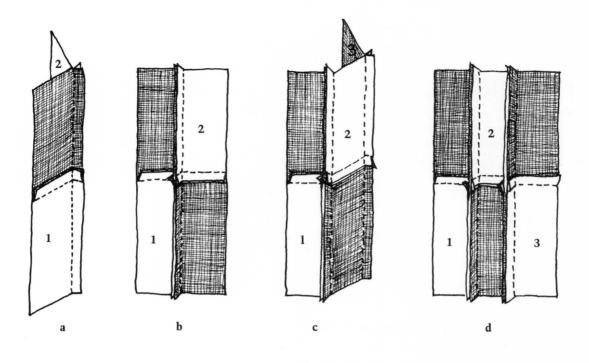

1–6. Seams are finger-pressed toward the left, as they are sewn.

Now that you have finished your first sample, it is a good idea to observe whether the finished segments are more or less than 1 inch wide. For the purpose of these samples, the exact width is not critical. However, you will need to take your seam width into account when planning future projects.

You will notice that the seaming produces a rich surface texture that gives the appearance of quilting without the handwork involved in quilting. The rippling of the fabric caused by the seaming will shorten the finished band a bit, if the pattern is composed entirely of very narrow segments. You may need to allow for an extra segment or two when planning a long pattern-band.

Since the table surface of the sewing machine lies to the left of the presser foot, this is a good place to lay out the seg-ments; you can easily pick up the piece nearest to the presser foot. This system enables you to visualize the row of cut segments moving one by one toward the needle of the machine from the left, being successively sewn to the pattern-band and turned over, flowing away again from the needle toward the left.

Keeping the band of sewn segments on top as you work permits you to see the previous seam as you sew, thus enabling you to check the width of the segment being sewn. It also facilitates pressing the seams in one direction. Furthermore, it is easier to handle the band of sewn segments when it is on top of the single flat segment under the presser foot. Later, when you have become familiar with the method of arranging and marking the segments in the order to be sewn, you may prefer to stack them in piles or develop your own system.

PATTERN #2

To make the second pattern take ten of the segments and set the rest aside.

1. Lay ten segments in a row, right side up, with the dark colors at the bottom. Figure 1–7 shows how alternate segments are slid up or down, forming the pattern.

2. Following Figure 1–8, mark the even-numbered segments with a pin on the right-hand edge, 1 inch below the seam. Mark the odd-numbered ones 1 inch above the seam. (The pin on the first segment may be omitted.)

3. Place Segment # 1, right side down, over Segment # 2, matching the seam to the pin on # 2. Pin in position and sew along the right-hand edge, as shown in Figure 1–9a. Finger-press seam to the left, as shown in Figure 1–9b.

4. Place this patch of two segments, right side down, on Segment # 3, matching the seam of # 2 to the pin on # 3. See Figure 1–9c. Sew as before and finger-press seam to the left. Your patch of three segments now looks like Figure 1–9d.

5. Match the seam of the right edge of Segment # 3 to the pin on # 4. Sew and finger-press as before. Continue in this manner until all segments are sewn, matching the seam of the last segment sewn to the pin on the next one, and alternately matching the seam to the dark color and to the light color. Press lightly on the back so that all seams lie in one direction.

6. To trim the edges of the finished pattern-band lay it on the table or the ironing board and line a straightedge or transparent ruler across the horizontal seams of the Segments # 1, 3, 5, 7, and 9. Pin the band to the board. Measure up from each end of the ruler 3¼ inches, as shown in Figure 1–10, and mark. Draw a line across the top, connecting the two marks. Mark the lower edge of the band 2¼ inches below the line defined by the top edge of the ruler, and draw a line across the bottom of the band. Trim the edges by cutting along these lines. *It is important to center the pattern of any band in this manner before trimming, so that the edges will be parallel to the pattern, and not just to each other.*

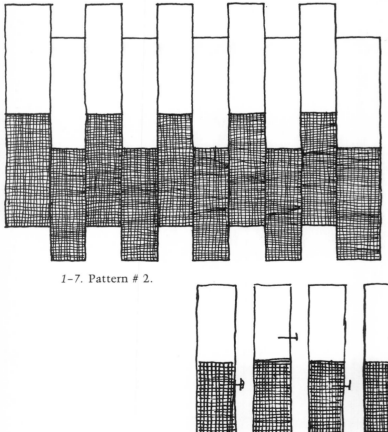

1-7. Pattern # 2.

1-8. Segments laid out in order, with the edges marked with pins for matching to the seams in the segments.

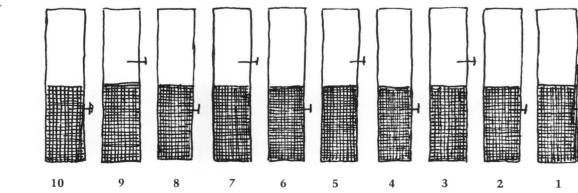

10   9   8   7   6   5   4   3   2   1

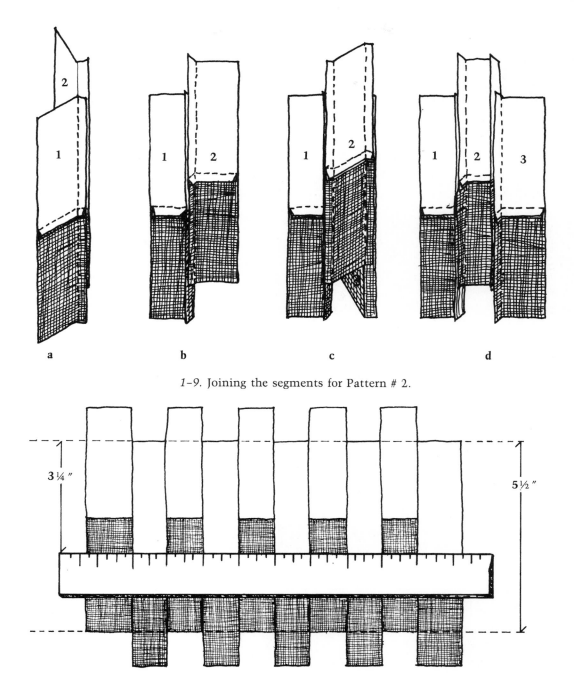

1-9. Joining the segments for Pattern # 2.

1-10. To make the edges of the band parallel to the center of pattern measure up and down from the top edge of a ruler laid across the horizontal seams.

A hint about seams: Notice that Figure 1-9 shows the horizontal seams of the segments pressed toward the dark color, in this case downward. It is desirable for the segments to be in this position (downward seam pressed toward you as you sit at the machine) so that the presser foot does not become entangled in the seaming. However, when the colors are reversed, this is not possible. If this should be a problem, you will find that some sort of flat tool, such as the bamboo point turner, will be helpful in feeding the fabric under the presser foot. It also helps to prevent the top segment from being dragged out of place.

PATTERN #3

To make the third pattern take the remaining ten segments. In this pattern (see Figure 1–11) you will reverse the colors, as you did for the first sample, and *also* slide the segments up and down as for the second sample.

1. Lay the last ten segments in a row, right side up, and mark them alternately 1 inch above and 1 inch below the seam, as shown in Figure 1–12. All the pins should be on the dark color.

2. Sew segments together in the same manner as for Pattern # 2, matching the seam of Segment # 1 to the pin on # 2, seam of # 2 to pin on # 3, and so on, until all of the segments have been sewn. Press seams lightly in one direction. Trim the edges according to the instructions previously given.

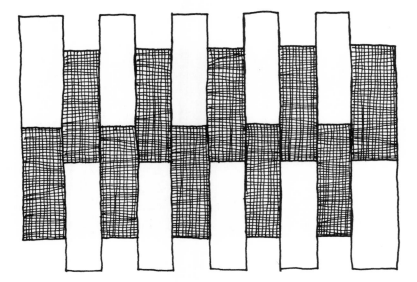

1–11. Pattern # 3.

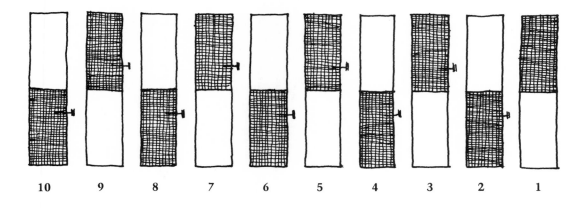

| 10 | 9 | 8 | 7 | 6 | 5 | 4 | 3 | 2 | 1 |

1–12. Segments laid out in order, with the edges marked for joining.

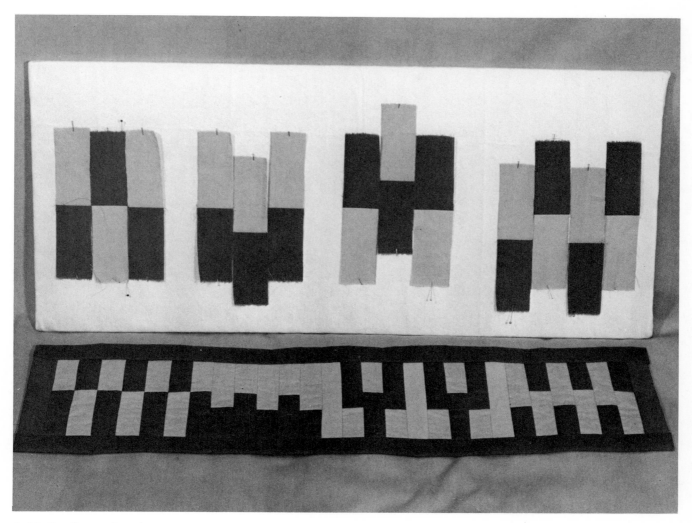

1–13. Small samples of Patterns # 1, # 2, and # 3 are joined to make a decorative panel. The third and fourth patterns at the right are variations of Pattern # 3; in one, light-colored insertions between groups of three segments form the dark-colored motifs, and in the other, the colors are reversed.

In case you have made all three sample bands and are one of those people who can't stand to see anything go to waste, Figure 1–13 will show you how to combine them to make an interesting band.

The next three samples are made with segments cut vertically just like the first three. But, because of the way the segments are joined, they form diagonal patterns. Because diagonal patterns require longer segments, you will need to prepare wider strips for these.

Tear a strip from each color 4½ inches wide (instead of 3½ inches) and sew and press as before. Mark and cut thirty segments 1½ inches wide, according to the instructions given for the first strip-band on page 14.

PATTERN #4

For this pattern (see Figure 1-14) take ten segments and put the rest aside.

1. Arrange the segments as shown in Figure 1-15, with the dark color at the bottom, and staggered. Mark each segment 1 inch below the seam with a pin, as shown in Figure 1-16. Although the drawing shows them numbered, it is not necessary to arrange these segments in numerical order, since they are marked and arranged identically.
2. Sew the segments together just as for the first three patterns, matching the seam of the first segment to the pin on the next and keeping the completed work on top. When all are joined, press the band and lay it face up on the board, making sure it lies straight.

Lay a ruler across the top or bottom of the points formed in the pattern to establish a center line, and mark it with two or three pins. Mark up and down from this line to make the outer edges parallel to the center of the band, and cut off the points at the edges, as shown in Figure 1-17.
3. To make the ends straight cut the band vertical to the center at one end, as shown in Figure 1-17, and sew the scrap onto the other end just as you would another segment. You will then have a rectangular piece, as shown in Figure 1-14.

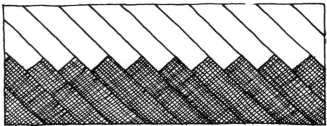

1-14. Pattern # 4.

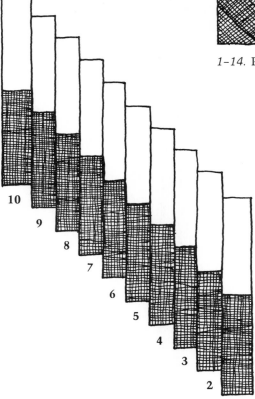

1-15. Segments arranged to make the pattern.

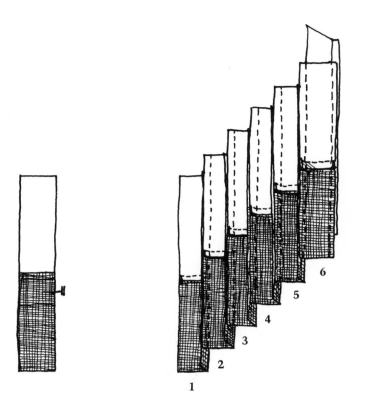

1-16. Mark each segment 1 inch below the seam as shown. Match the seam of the first segment to the pin on the next, and so on.

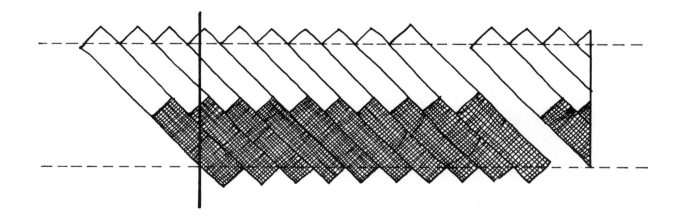

1-17. To make the ends of the pattern band straight mark one end with a vertical line, cut it, and sew the piece to the other end of the band.

PATTERN #5

To make this pattern (see Figure 1–18) take ten segments and put the rest aside.

1. Arrange the segments as you did for Pattern # 1, reversing the dark and light, and stagger them as you did for # 4. See Figure 1–19. Mark each segment 1 inch above the seam, as shown in Figure 1–20, and sew together in the usual manner, matching the seam of Segment # 1 to the pin on Segment # 2, and so on.

2. When all are joined, mark the outer edges parallel to the center of the band and cut off the points. Straighten the ends by cutting off one end and sewing it onto the other as for Pattern # 4.

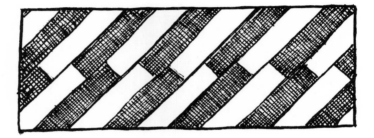

1–18. Pattern # 5.

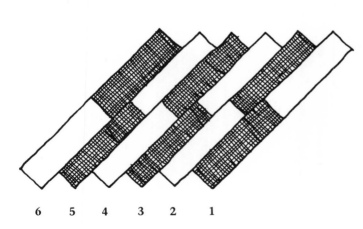

6 5 4 3 2 1

1–19. Segments arranged to make the pattern.

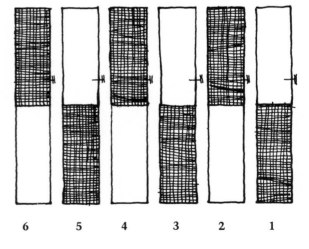

6 5 4 3 2 1

1–20. Segments laid out in order of sewing, with edges marked for joining.

PATTERN #6

For this last pattern (see Figure 1-21) take the remaining ten segments.

1. Arrange the segments with the dark color at the bottom and stagger them, as shown in Figure 1-22. Pin alternate segments 1 inch below the seam on the dark color, and pin the others 2 inches above the seam on the light color, as shown in Figure 1-23. Match the seam of one to the pin on the next, as before, and sew together. When all are joined, press lightly on the back and trim the edges according to the instructions previously given.

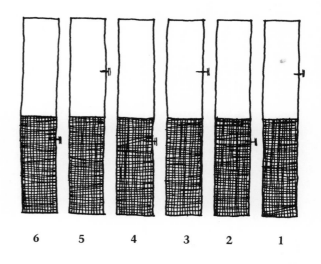

6   5   4   3   2   1

1-23. Segments laid out in order, with edges marked for joining.

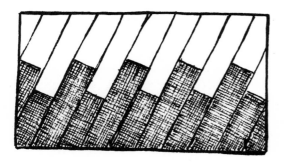

1-21. Pattern # 6.

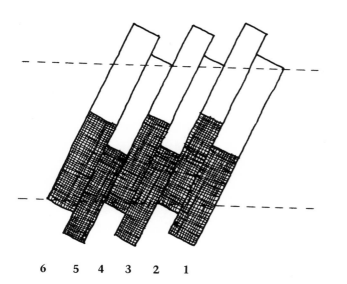

6   5   4   3   2   1

1-22. Segments arranged to make the pattern.

When segments are added one at a time, according to the system recommended, the group of sewn segments is drawn out each time from under the presser foot so that it can be placed over the segment being added. This wastes thread as well as time. It has been suggested that the segments be joined two at a time in a continuous string, then into groups of four, and so forth, to avoid wasting thread. However, these bunches of segments can be difficult to manage. A better solution is to divide the segments into two lots, adding a segment to one lot and then to the other. For example, sew together two segments, and, without pulling out the thread and cutting it, join a second pair of segments. Cut off the first pair of segments and join it to a new segment, then cut off the second pair, and so forth. The two bands can be sewn together when all are joined.

23

1-24. The finished results of Patterns # 4, # 5, and
6. The zigzag pattern in the center is a popular
one and is much more attractive when made smaller
and narrower. As can be seen, diagonal patterns can be
made using segments cut vertically.

In the next chapter, which shows several authentic Seminole pattern-bands and how to make them, you will notice a preponderance of diagonal patterns, both those made of diagonally cut segments and those made with vertical segments, as shown in Figure 1-24. Diagonal patterns tend to be more active and lively than patterns consisting of vertical and horizontal lines, and this exuberant effect is further emphasized by the brilliance and variety of the colors favored by the Seminoles.

2

TYPICAL SEMINOLE PATTERNS AND HOW TO MAKE THEM

In many ways the sewing machine is one of the most revolutionary inventions of recent times, and the history of its development is an intriguing story. The first sewing machine to be used commercially was patented in Britain at the beginning of the nineteenth century and was made for embroidering on fabric. It took years of unremitting effort by numerous contributors to perfect a practical machine that would sew two pieces of cloth together. It is ironic that today the sewing machine's efficiency in doing just that has overshadowed its potential as a tool of the decorative arts.

The Seminole Indian women began using the sewing machine sometime in the 1890s to create the colorful decorative bands that are an integral part of their costume. Considering the fact that they sewed their intricate patchwork on the small portable hand-cranked models then available, we can only wonder what these craftswomen might have accomplished had they had access to today's versatile and highly sophisticated home sewing machines. This distinctive form of tribal art, strip patchwork, may be unique for its use of modern technological tools and materials. Yet it is not an altogether surprising development in view of the Seminole people's propensity to adopt whatever they found useful and desirable in the culture of the British and American settlers.

Present-day Seminole costume is characterized by the use of a nearly limitless array of color and a great variety of pattern-bands in a single garment. In earlier times, the skirts of the women and the knee-length shirts of the men were usually made of printed calicos in dark or quiet colors. These were embellished above the hemline with borders of appliquéd braids and strips of colored cloth in geometric patterns. It seems probable that these patterns evolved from the ribbon work that was practiced by many Indian tribes, including those of the southeastern states.

Historical paintings of the Seminole leaders show the knee-length tunics with single borders at the hem. In other examples we see the men's dresses banded from yoke to hem with strips of colored cloth in varying widths, interspersed with bands of patchwork in simple, striking patterns. A long shirt of the 1830s seen in the Denver Art Museum was made of red cotton calico and trimmed from waist to hem with four decorative bands. Three of them were of patchwork in blue and white, and a fourth (second from bottom) was a pleated ruffle of blue and white calico. The patchwork bands and narrow plain-bands were sewn onto the garments and can be thought of as appliquéd.

The ancestors of the Seminoles (the Creeks) had lived in close contact with the white settlers from precolonial times and had ample opportunity to become familiar with patchwork. Patchwork originated in the New World because of the scarcity of materials and the necessity to patch the quilts brought from Europe to preserve their usefulness. Sometime in the late 1890s the Seminole women began to buy portable hand-cranked sewing machines at the trading posts, and, not long after that, the styles of their clothing began to change. Patchwork replaced appliqué around the year 1910, and, when World War I made printed calicos from Germany unavailable, many of the garments became more elaborate. There were more pattern-bands in the men's shirts and the women's skirts, and narrower strips and segments, which resulted in fine patterns with very tiny pieces. This was probably done to compensate for the lack of patterned fabrics. In the thirties the men adopted pants and the shirt was shortened to the style Seminole men wear today.

Contemporary skirts and shirts usually have from three to five pattern-bands, but sometimes a skirt may have as many as seven. Each of these bands is different in design, and each is inserted between narrow-bands of various plain colors. These are then sewn between wider bands of one plain color which forms the background color of the garment. Narrow strips of folded fabric or of rickrack braid are added to the plain body-bands as additional embellishment. The garments are never lined, and all the seaming can be seen on the reverse side.

Traditionally, each pattern-band is usually made of different colors, and contrasting colors are used in the narrow-bands to which they are attached, creating an effect of vitality and exuberance. The list of colors used appears to represent the full range of colors likely to have been available in the firm, finely woven cotton fabric. The favorite colors appear to be red and yellow with black, and pale green and mauve are preferred over pink and blue. Black is most often used as the foundation color, but blue, green, and red are also popular. White, however, is never used for the body of the garment, although it appears often in the pattern-bands and in the narrow plain-bands.

These pattern-bands are always used horizontally and evidently are specially designed to be viewed in this position. It is not known whether this has any traditional meaning. In former times, the colors on the yoke of the shirt identified the wearer's family, but nowhere have I discovered any mention of the possible symbolic significance of the patterns themselves. It seems feasible that the basic character of the patterns that have developed since 1900 has been dictated by the use of the sewing machine, since it would be impossible to achieve these patterns without it.

Although some of the motifs appear to be quite intricate, they are actually the outcome of clever planning and a sensible use of the strip-sewing method. They show great ingenuity and skillful workmanship. These patterns are never recorded, but are passed freely from person to person. At one time, though, on the Dania Reservation in Florida, certain patterns were occasionally reserved for one woman's exclusive use.

Some of the garments studied have been sewn entirely with white thread, including the colored appliquéd strips. Others have been sewn with a mixture of thread colors, and matching threads were used on the appliquéd strips. The length of the stitches generally varied from 12 to 16 per inch, although in a small apron with some very fine patchwork, the length of the stitches ranged from 18 to 22 per inch. In this apron very narrow strips and segments had been used, and in one of the pattern-bands there were pieces that measured $1/8$ by $3/8$ inch on the surface of the garment. Close inspection of this apron also revealed that sometimes the very narrow strips within the segment were achieved by taking a second, deeper seam in the strip-band after it had been sewn once, the result being that several thicknesses of cloth overlapped where the segments were joined.

Strip patchwork is not in any way limited to the types of designs developed by the Seminoles. In fact, the design possibilities are virtually limitless. Yet, by studying some typical Seminole patterns, you will learn more about the technique itself.

The colors in the three bands shown in the apron in Figure 2–1 are totally unrelated to each

2-1. A Seminole apron with three typical pattern-bands.

other. Yet, they are unified by the colors used in the bands that enclose them and by the narrow strips of appliqué. The top band is 1 inch wide (pattern section only) when finished, and the two lower ones are each 1¼ inches wide.

The colors in the top band are purple and yellow, with a bright blue strip above, and a white below. At quick glance it would appear that this pattern-band is similar to Pattern # 4. They are different, however, in that the triangular tips on this band are not 90-degree angles, but rather 60-degree angles. You will need to construct a cardboard template in the form of a parallelogram with 60-degree angles for mark-

ing the segments at the required angle. See Figure 2–2. Since these are to be 1 ³/₈ inches wide before sewing, it would be convenient to make the template that width or perhaps just a shade narrower to allow for the width of the line drawn on the fabric.

Make the top strip-band, using strips of purple and yellow fabric 1½ inches wide. For a finished band about 22 inches long, each strip needs to be about 30 inches in length. After cutting the segments as shown in Figure 2–2, mark each right-hand edge with a pin, ³/₈ inch from the bottom. Now match the seam of one segment to the pin on the next. Trim the edges as

27

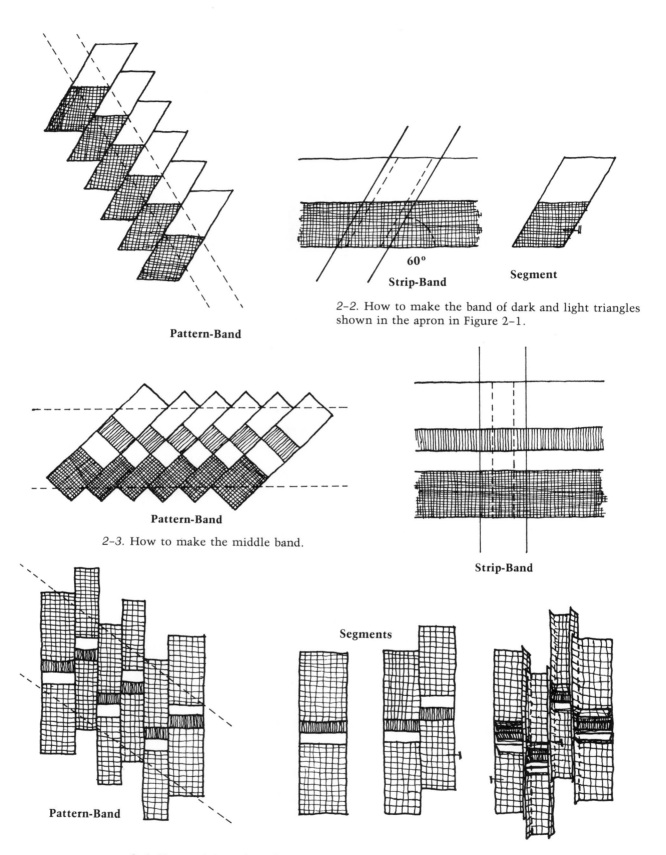

Pattern-Band

60°

Strip-Band **Segment**

2-2. How to make the band of dark and light triangles shown in the apron in Figure 2-1.

Pattern-Band

Strip-Band

2-3. How to make the middle band.

Segments

Pattern-Band

2-4. How to join and mark the segments for the bottom band.

28

described in Chapter 1, and add the narrow plain-bands. These are $^7/_8$ inch wide when finished—a bright blue above and a white below.

Note: Colors used are given only as an example of the typical use of color. Should you prefer to use different colors when duplicating these bands, note the distribution of the dark and light values, as this is the factor that determines the effectiveness of the pattern.

The middle band in this apron is an elaboration of Pattern # 4, the difference being that it is made up of four strips. The colors are yellow, emerald green, white, and red, from top to bottom. The yellow and red strips are each 1¼ inches wide, and the green and white ones are each 1 inch wide. Make the band about 33 inches long, and cut it into segments 1 inch wide. Because, when laying out the pattern-band, you merely slide each segment up from left to right so that the corners of the green squares meet, no marking is necessary. See Figure 2–3. The plain-bands on either side of this band are bright blue above and light green below and are $^3/_8$ inch wide when finished.

For the bottom band make a strip-band using two strips of coral pink, each 1¾ inches wide, and one each of chartreuse and bright blue, each ¾ inch wide. All should be 33 inches long. Segments are cut 1 inch wide; alternate segments are reversed and every two segments are sewn together so that the small blue pieces meet at the corners. Mark each patch of two segments on the right-hand edge, ¾ inch below the seam joining the blue to the coral, and join the patches as you did the segments, matching the seam on the top patch to the pin on the bottom one, as shown in Figure 2–4. Trim the edges as shown.

This band has a narrow green band above it and a white one below. Note that white was used below the top pattern-band, and in the middle pattern-band itself. The bright blue of the lower pattern-band was repeated in the plain-bands above the two others, and the chartreuse echoed the yellow used in the two upper pattern-bands.

It can be seen that the plain-bands have several functions. They are used to set off the colors in the pattern-bands, and to finish them and make them appear wider. More impor-

tantly, they provide a means of unifying the sometimes disparate colors in the pattern-bands, which often are made up in advance to be rolled up and set aside for future use.

The top band in the apron shown in Figure 2–5 is the same as that in Figure 2–1, except that the light and dark values are reversed. The colors are bright blue and yellow; the plain-band above is pale aqua and the one below is medium purple. The second band was also made in the same way, except that a narrow strip of white was added to the strip-band between the red and blue. Bright yellow above and light turquoise below finish this band.

For the bottom band make a strip-band 45 inches long, using a strip of black 1 $^3/_8$ inches wide, chartreuse ¾ inch wide, red ¾ inch wide, and aqua 1¾ inches wide. Sew these together in that order from top to bottom and cut into vertical segments 1 inch wide. Reverse alternate segments and sew together in patches of two, so that the small red pieces meet at the corners. Mark each patch ¼ inch above the seam on the right-hand edge, as shown in Figure 2–6, and join in the usual manner. This band has a white band above, about $^5/_8$ inch wide, and a dark maroon below.

Notice that the top pattern-band in the skirt shown in Figure 2–7 is the same as Pattern # 5. The colors are red and light turquoise blue, each 1¾ inches wide. Fabric 45 inches wide, cut into $^7/_8$-inch segments, will yield about fifty and will make a band about 25 inches long. So, for the skirt, at least three strip-bands would be needed. Reverse the segments as before and mark each segment on the right-hand edge, $^3/_8$ inch above the seam. Sew segments together and trim the edge. This pattern-band is much more attractive when made smaller than the sample pattern, and is about 1¼ inches wide when finished.

Although the middle band is made in a way very similar to the band in Figure 2–6, it has a curiously ambiguous, meandering effect, quite unlike the clearly seen pattern in the small apron. Alternate segments were reversed, but, instead of having the black squares meet at the corners, they have been slid apart so that the light colors (yellow and chartreuse) are connected and surround the black squares, as shown in Figure 2–8. The ambiguity is

2-5. This apron also utilizes typical Seminole patterns. The top band is the same as the one taught in Figure 2-2. The middle band is similar, except that a narrow strip of white was added to the strip-band to give a different emphasis to the pattern. The bottom band is very much like the bottom band of the apron in Figure 2-1, but, because of the way the colors are arranged and the segments are joined, the effect is very different.

2-6. How the segments are joined to make the bottom band in Figure 2-5.

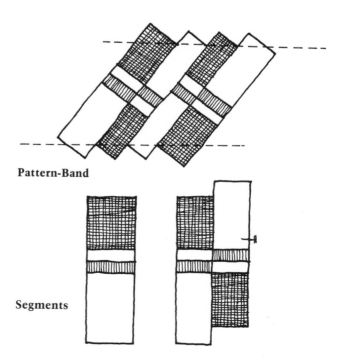

Pattern-Band

Segments

heightened by the fact that this band has been sewn with purposeful carelessness; the strips and the segments vary in width, and the intervals between the black squares are inconsistent in width, which only makes the band more intriguing.

30

2-7. Three pattern-bands in a typical Seminole skirt. Notice the narrow strips of appliqué that were added below each of the bands. They make the bands appear wider than they actually are.

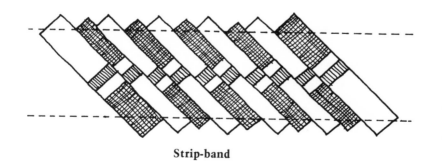

Strip-band

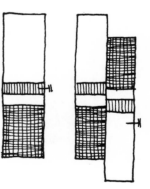

Segments

2-8. The segments in the middle band of Figure 2-7 are just like those in the lower band in Figure 2-5, but the way the white spaces are slid past each other when the segments are joined changes the pattern remarkably.

Colors used in the bottom band are maroon, warm yellow, royal blue, and white. The maroon and white on the outer edges are 1½ inches wide before sewing, and the blue and yellow are ¾ inch wide. Make a template as you would for the top band in Figure 2-1 and mark the segments at a 60-degree angle, $1\frac{1}{8}$ inches wide, to make segments $\frac{5}{8}$ inch wide when sewn together. See Figure 2-2. Slide each segment down, from left to right, so that the upper seam of the yellow strip meets the lower seam of the blue, or, let it be just a little below, as in the photograph. Fabric 45 inches wide will yield about thirty-eight segments and will make a band about 26 inches long when sewn. See Figure 2-9.

In this skirt there is one plain-band above each pattern-band. These range from ¾ inch to 1 inch wide. There are two plain-bands below each pattern-band, varying in width from ½ to 1 inch, and on each of the lower plain-bands a narrow strip of appliqué has been sewn. Above the first two pattern-bands the narrow plain-bands are white, repeating the white used in the lower pattern-band. Greens, reds, and yellows are used in the plain-bands and strips of appliqué in such a way that all the pattern-bands are held together visually. The addition of these bands and narrow strips makes these pattern-bands appear much wider than their actual width of 1¾ inches.

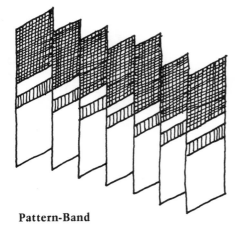

Pattern-Band

2-9. Segments joined to make the bottom band in Figure 2-7.

In the well-designed apron shown in Figure 2-10, the colors have been limited to red, medium (slightly bluish) green, pale yellow, black, white, and one narrow band of cool medium brown, which is used at the lower edge of the band of vertical bars. The body of the apron is dark navy blue. One-half inch strips of red are sewn above the first, second, and fourth pattern-bands, repeating the red used in the third pattern-band. White and yellow are judiciously distributed throughout the design, and the green used in the top band appears again in the narrow appliqué strips and in the plain-bands.

Note that the top pattern-band is similar to the bottom pattern-band in Figure 2-7, except that the darks and lights are arranged differently. The colors are green, black, white, and red from top to bottom. The plain-band above it is red, the one below it a quiet yellow, and the narrow strip of appliqué on the body-band below this is green.

For the band of vertical bars, tear two strips of yellow and two of black, one inch wide and about 32 inches long. Sew these into a strip-band of four stripes and press it. Cut this piece in half across the stripes and join the pieces side by side; again, cut in half and join the two pieces. See Figure 2-11. Continue until you have a narrow band about 2 inches wide and 32 inches long. The plain-bands are red above, cool brown below, with a white strip appliquéd above on the body-band, and a red one appliquéd below.

A long narrow band of vertical bars, made in the same manner as the one shown in Figure 2-11, is used in making the patches for the third band. Join a 24-inch-long strip of white ¾ inch wide to one of red 1½ inches wide, each 24 inches long, and follow the directions given for the previous band. Trim this band to 1¾ inches wide as in Step 1, Figure 2-12. To each side sew a ¾-inch strip of white, and, to one side of this, a $\frac{7}{8}$-inch strip of red. See Step 2. Press, and mark the segments 1¼ inches wide, as shown in Step 3. To make the segments needed to complete the patch, tear a strip of white 1½ inches wide and one of red 1¼ inches wide, both 24 inches long. After sewing, press and cut into vertical segments ¾ inch wide. For the plain red insertions use a strip 2¼ inches

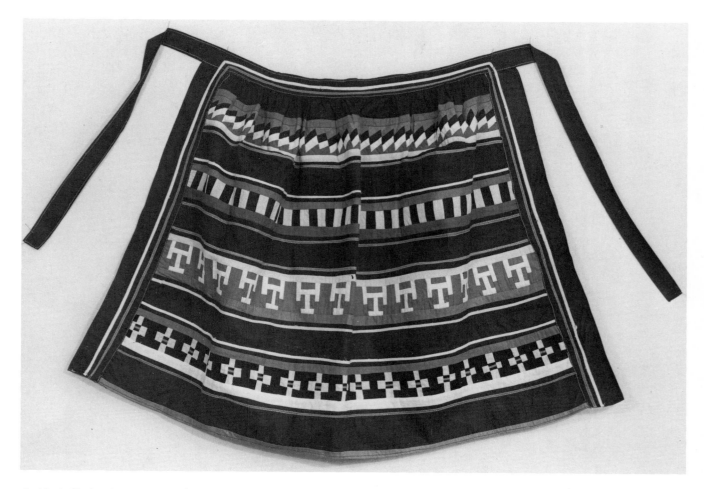

2–10. A distinctive apron with some interesting composite patterns.

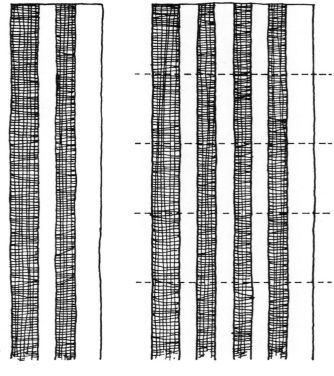

Pattern-Band

2–11. How to make the band of vertical bars in Figure 2–10.

Strip-Band

wide and about 34 inches long, cut into segments 1¼ inches wide. Assemble the pattern-band according to Figure 2–12. The plain-band above is yellow and the one below is green, with appliqué strips of green above and yellow below.

To make the motif for the bottom band, tear the strips as follows: two 36-inch-long black, one 36-inch-long yellow, two 18-inch-long yellow, and one 18-inch-long black, all to be 1

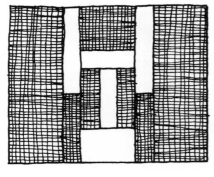

Patch

2-12. How to make the motifs in the third band.

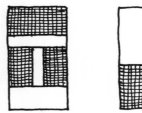

Pattern-Band

Pattern-Band Plus Strips

Segments   **Insertion**

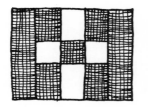

Patch

2-13. How to make the bottom band.

Segments

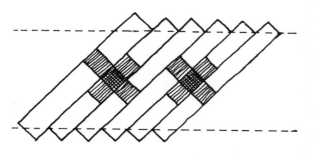

Pattern-Band

2-14. A variation of Figure 2–13.

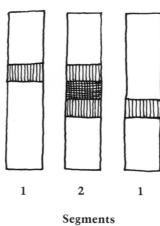

1   2   1

Segments

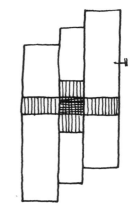

Segments Pinned

2-15. These dolls from the Dania Reservation in Hollywood, Florida, are wearing dresses embellished with small-scale pattern-bands and rows of fine rickrack braid.

inch wide. Join the 36-inch strips, placing the yellow in the center of the strip-band. Join the 18-inch strips, placing black in the center. (On the apron shown, a narrow strip of red has been sewn down the center of the black center strip. If you wish to follow this example, be careful to stretch the band itself gently as you sew on this narrow strip, to avoid puckering.) Cut both bands into 1-inch segments and assemble into patches, as shown in Figure 2–13. For the insertions which separate the motifs, use a strip of black 2 inches wide and 20 inches long, and cut into 1-inch segments. The plain-bands are red above, about ½ inch wide, and white below, about ¾ inch wide. The upper strip of appliqué is white, and the lower one is red.

Notice that the strip-bands used in Figures 2–4, 2–6, 2–8, and 2–9 are strikingly similar. The variety of patterns that can result from slight changes in the position of the colors or values in the strip-band or from a slight shift in the arrangement of segments, illustrates the limitless possibilities for innovation offered by the strip patchwork technique.

Shown in Figure 2–14 is an attractive variation of the motif shown in Figure 2–13. Made in orange and brown on a beige background and separated with beige insertions, it resembles a Brown-eyed Susan. For both examples it is easy to see that one strip-band needs to be twice as long as the other because you will be using twice as many of its segments. Use a strip of beige 1¾ inches wide and another 2¾ inches wide, with a 1-inch strip of orange in the center for the longer band. For the shorter, use two strips of beige 1¾ inches wide, two of orange 1 inch wide, and one of brown 1 inch wide.

Cut the bands into vertical segments 1 inch wide, and reverse half of those cut from the longer band. Assemble into patches of three, matching the brown square in the center to the orange squares. To join the patches mark the right-hand edge 1 inch above the orange square and sew to the insertions as shown, matching the seam below the orange square to the pin.

Dolls, like the ones shown in Figure 2–15, as

well as aprons and other articles can be purchased at the Seminole Indian Village on the Dania Reservation near Hollywood, Florida, and also at the Miami Airport. The Museum Gift Center of the Historical Association of Southern Florida in Miami has a full line of dolls and clothing. Examples of Seminole clothing may be seen at the Plume Indian Museum between Monroe and Highland Hills, New York, and at the Denver Art Museum.

The pattern in the skirt of the doll at the right in the photograph is a popular one. Figure 2–16 shows the segments needed to make these small patches. Several variations of this motif are shown in Chapter 6. (When making bands of diagonal squares with corners touching, a convenient way to assemble them that also saves material is shown in Figure 2–17.)

Another pattern that is often seen in Seminole bands is shown in Figure 2–18. Here are the steps for making it:

Step 1. Make a long band of vertical stripes, in the manner described and shown in Figure 2–11.

Step 2. Add strips to each side.

Step 3. Cut into segments and join with corners touching.

Although none of the garments shown in this chapter have included the diamond pattern, directions for making it are given here because it is useful and attractive (see Figure 2–19a, b, c).

1. Make a strip-band of three strips and mark it with a line at any angle desired.
2. Place pins at the top and bottom of the center strip ¼ inch from this line, as shown, to denote the seamline. (Be sure to measure these seam allowances vertical to the first line drawn, and not along the line of the sewn strip, or they will be narrower than ¼ inch.)
3. To make diamonds with equal sides measure the distance between the two pins and make the adjacent sides of the diamond the same length, marking them with pins. Add seam allowance.
4. Make a cardboard template the width of the segment thus defined, and use it for marking the segments.

Notice that by sliding each segment *down* from left to right a band of vertical diamonds is formed. To make a longer and narrower band of horizontal diamonds, slide the segments *up* from left to right.

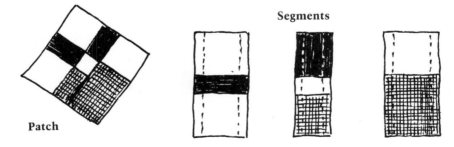

Segments

Patch

2–16. Segments needed to make the strip-band shown on the doll on the right in Figure 2–15.

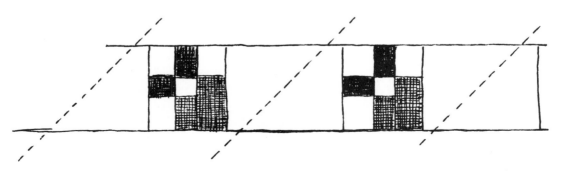

2–17. How to join the patches to make the band of diagonal squares with corners touching.

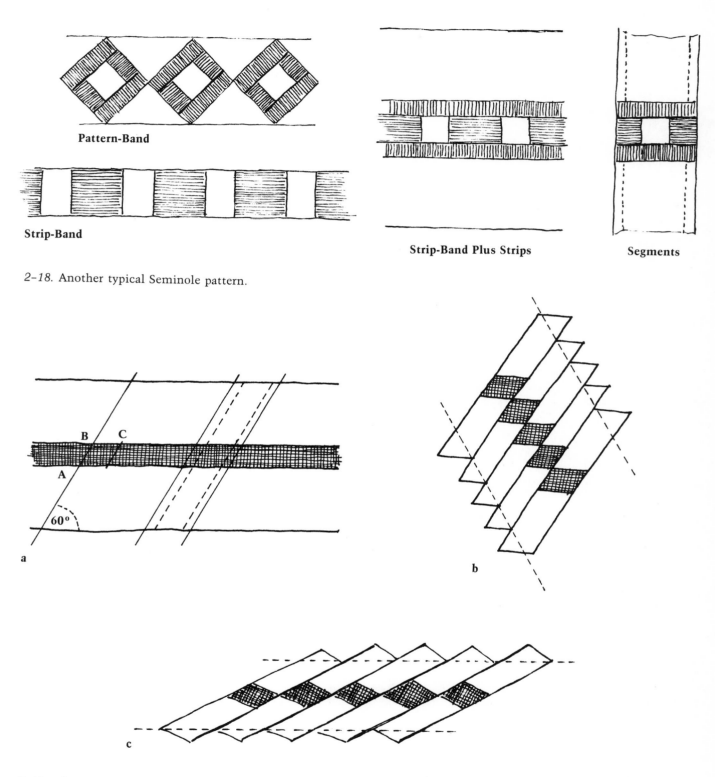

Pattern-Band

Strip-Band

Strip-Band Plus Strips

Segments

2-18. Another typical Seminole pattern.

B **C**

A

60°

a

b

c

2-19 a, b, c. How to make bands with diamond patterns. Notice the difference in the patterns, depending upon which way the segments are slid.

DESIGNING FOR STRIP PATCHWORK

Working with the simple geometric shapes of Seminole patchwork has led me to a deeper understanding of the relationship between pattern and color, and it is my hope that you will share this experience with me. Intricate designs have a fascination of their own, but, for the purposes of the designer, they are relatively unimportant. Patterns are composed of combinations of the same few basic shapes, but the combinations can be varied infinitely. For example, a lovely Japanese kimono achieves a stunning effect by combining a delicate floral pattern in pastel colors on a white background with areas of bold black-and-white checkerboard squares.

Even the most casual examination of ethnic textiles impresses us with the prevalence of geometric patterns incorporated. Without knowing more about the given culture, it is impossible to identify most of these patterns or motifs by themselves. For instance, the motif seen in a piece of machine-made embroidery from India can also be found in Oriental carpets, in Northwest Indian baskets, and in the Early American quilt block seen in countless variations and known by many names. See Figure 3–1.

In many traditional works these motifs have particular meanings. Often the ways in which

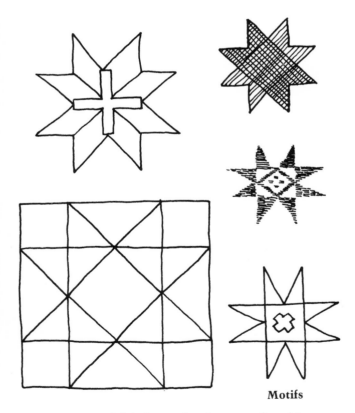

Motifs

3–1. Versions of this four-pointed star are found in Northwest Indian basketry, Oriental carpets, patchwork quilts, embroidered and woven textiles, and many other artifacts, demonstrating the universal appeal of geometric motifs.

they may be used are limited. Their form is also influenced by the materials and techniques employed; embroidery permits greater freedom than does weaving, for example. We are unhampered by any prescriptions or prohibitions in the use of these motifs, so we are free to select and employ them for purely formal reasons, to fit them into our designs as needed. Yet, oddly enough, we are all aware of having certain favorite figures, of having powerful preferences for the circle, the triangle, or some other shape. Is this because we like the look of a particular shape and how it works in our design, or is there possibly an inner urge that causes us to produce these shapes as opposed to others? Surely this phenomenon attests to the fact that even the simplest geometric figures have expressive value. Furthermore, almost everyone who engages in making something, for whatever purpose, seems to be inclined to add a bit of embellishment to it. Is this to satisfy an innate human need, or is it simply a natural function, like breathing?

But pattern, lines and shapes of dark and light juxtaposed, is only a part of our concern. The use of color has a crucial effect upon the use of the strip-sewing technique, since many other things besides horizontal pattern-bands in brilliant colors can be made by the technique. Similar patterns, done in black, white, and brown, acquire an ''African'' look; two strongly contrasting values can result in a snappy contemporary design; colors closely related in hue and value can fashion a quiet pattern very different in effect from the traditional Seminole bands.

Although the variety of colors employed in typical Seminole garments is at times almost bewildering, the distribution of dark and light values is skillfully handled, and the various patterns are unified by the selection of colors overall. One could hazard a number of reasons for the Seminole way of using color; suffice it to remark that it is uninhibited, exuberant, and unquestionably distinctive.

If one limits the colors in a Seminole pattern to only two, simple geometric shapes emerge—bars, squares, triangles, diamonds, and zigzags—as seen in Figure 3–2. To make the example shown, two different strip-bands of navy blue and vermilion were made. These

were cut into 1-inch segments (½ inch wide when sewn), and were arranged into simple patterns often seen in Seminole bands, each one producing a very different effect. Notice how dissimilar the bands of bars and crosses appear in the apron in Figure 2–10. They appear different not only because of the number of colors used, but because of the manner in which they are used.

Soft woodsy tones of blues and greens, with a touch of brown and gold, were used in the pillow shown in Figure 3–3. Designed to fit the specific color requirements of the owner, it shows how effectively a single shape and a limited palette of colors can be employed.

A template was made in the shape of the sawtooth triangle (see Figure 3–4), and the pieces were cut from bands of two colors as required by the design. These pieces were then joined end to end, and the resulting bands sewn together without the usual narrow edging bands, which required careful matching of the corners. This was not difficult, since the pieces were cut on the bias and the pillow was made of wool, which stretches easily. Because pillows are subjected to considerable stress, it is recommended that a good-quality cotton-wrapped polyester thread be used for sewing, as it has considerable stretch built into it, and is very

3–2. Simple shapes such as these squares, crosses, and bars emerge when strip-bands are limited to two colors.

3–3. The basic sawtooth band was used to make this pillow in soft, closely related colors, and bears little resemblance to the original Seminole pattern. Pillow by the author.

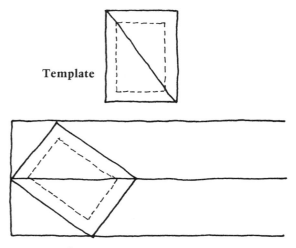

Template

Strip-Band

3-4. Pattern for making the pillow in Figure 3-3.

strong. To make a similar pillow, use colored felt-tipped pens to draw a plan of your design, and count the number of pieces of each color combination needed.

Even with color and value contrast almost totally eliminated, a rich and pleasing surface can be created from strips of wool joined by the strip technique. The pillow shown in Figure 3–5 is done in cream and pale oatmeal colors. Because woolen fabrics are bulky, it is recommended that the seams be made ½-inch wide and pressed open. Step-by-step directions for making similar pillows of wool are given in Chapter 5.

How well we know that it is difficult to appreciate a good design if the colors in it are repugnant to us, and that glorious or seductive colors can often redeem an otherwise unimpressive composition. Most of us are well

3–5. In another departure from the vivid colors and strong contrasts used by the Seminoles, this pillow of cream- and pale-oatmeal- colored wool shows how effectively closely keyed colors and values can be used in strip patchwork. Pillow by the author.

aware of the expressive aspect of color, but are less so of its constructive aspect. Color works in many ways to build underlying structure, to maintain coherence, to lend variety, and to produce rhythm and movement; much fine contemporary painting is concerned almost exclusively with the function of color.

For the textile craftsman, an understanding of color is probably more important than the mastering of spatial relationships. This may be because beautiful textiles make a specific appeal to our senses of color and texture, which is the reason why so many of us are drawn to stitchery, weaving, patchwork, and other fiber arts. It is also true that many of the technical limitations associated with the fiber arts are happily embraced by most of their practitioners; the use of color offers the best opportunity for individual expression. The discriminating use of color can distinguish a familiar pattern and raise it out of the ordinary; and, fortunately, using color effectively can be learned through thoughtful observation and a willingness to experiment.

The dynamic functions of color relationships are especially apparent in strip patchwork, which provides opportunities for some fascinating experiments with the properties of color.

When you analyze the components of Seminole patterns, you will become aware of the following variables. You might find these a useful guide when designing your own pattern-bands:

1. Number of colors used.
2. Number of strips in the strip-band.
3. Widths of strips in the strip-band.
4. Angle at which the segments are cut.
5. Widths of the segments.
6. Manner in which segments are joined.
7. The combining of segments from two or more strip-bands or the insertion of plain segments to form a part of a motif or to separate motifs.

You have already seen how limiting the number of colors changes a pattern markedly. The number of strips in a band may be increased with or without increasing the number of colors. When designing on your own, try bands of five strips, first using two colors, then three, four, and five, arranged in various patterns. Which combinations are more versatile? Try insertions of plain colors for further discoveries. Experiment with the widths of the strips and the widths of the segments to see how this affects the patterns. Have you cut the segments at different angles and of differing widths? You will observe that vertical segments can be used in many more combinations than can those cut on the diagonal.

Cut plain segments of one of the colors used in a strip-band and insert them between patches of multicolored segments. Then do the same with a different color in the band. What appeared to be the background color in one pattern may become the accent color in the other. Add various narrow-bands of a plain color to either side of your sample of segments and note the many changes that occur. You will discover many interesting patterns to incorporate into your own projects by doing a few systematic experiments.

Figure 3–6 shows a section of the strip-band used to make one of the pattern-bands in the Christmas tree hanging described in Chapter 8, with some of the ways in which it can be cut and arranged. Note that the strip-band is somewhat similar to those shown in Chapter 2, although the values are arranged differently and there is less contrast. The simple checkerboard of narrow segments, alternately slid up and down, was chosen to punctuate the grouping of diagonal patterns and gives a feeling of stability to the design.

See Figure 3–7. Plain insertions transform the chevron border at the left, done in yellow, orange, green, and dark brown, into a row of tulips. Note the rippling on the plain insertions, which were cut on the straight grain of the fabric. When segments are cut on the diagonal, the plain insertions should be cut on the same bias, as in the example on the right.

Identical patches of dark brown, cocoa, orange tones, and white are set into the T-shirts shown in Figure 3–8. One shirt is dark brown and the other is cocoa-colored. Notice the difference in the size, as well as in the pattern, because of the way the colors merge or contrast with the backgrounds. This principle can be used to make the straight edge of a pattern-band disappear, so that only a row of motifs is seen.

Striped materials offer interesting possibilities for strip patchwork. In addition to saving time and work, they can be used to make mundane fabrics considerably more interesting, as shown in the lively beach pillow in Figure 3–9 made of navy blue and yellow sailcloth.

When experimenting with design ideas, do not overlook the possibility of using printed fabrics. Not only prints with small figures, but some of those with large, bold patterns and bright colors that may not be especially pleasing in themselves, can be cut into strips and combined to create surprising and delightful designs. The interesting composition shown in Figure 3–10 was made of several different black-and-white printed fabrics, combined with strips of plain black, and a few small squares of plain black and plain white. It shows how patterned fabrics with strong contrast can be used with good effect in strip patchwork.

Although the handsome wall quilt shown in Figure 3–11 was not made strictly by the strip patchwork method, it or one very like it could easily have been so made. The striking, yet simple, design suggests many possibilities for making large-scale fabric murals using the strip technique.

These are just some ideas of what can be done with pattern and color. With the photographs in this chapter as inspiration, perhaps you are ready to think about designing your own pattern-bands.

I frequently hear a wistful comment from women who consistently occupy themselves with stitchery, needlepoint, quilting, or patch-

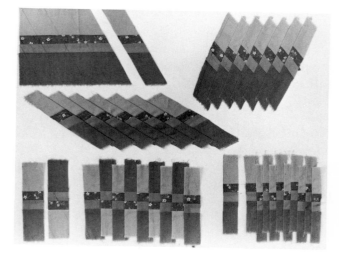

3-6. Shown here are some of the ways segments from one strip-band can be cut and joined to make different patterns. This band was used in the Christmas tree banner in Chapter 8.

3-9. An experiment with striped fabric resulted in this jazzy beach pillow of navy blue and bright yellow sailcloth. Pillow made by Kay Kelly.

3-7. Three examples of chevron borders. Along with the colors used, which are yellow, orange, leaf green, and dark brown, the plain insertions added to the band in the middle make it look like a row of tulips.

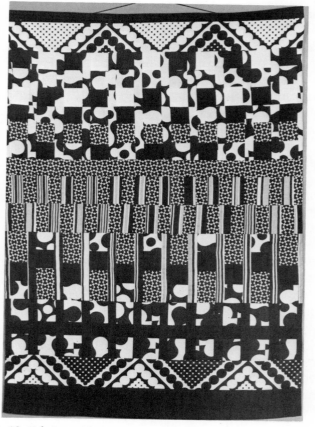

3-8. The two patches inserted in these T-shirts are identical, and combine dark brown, cocoa brown, orange, and white. In the cocoa-colored shirt at the left, the dark brown triangles are emphasized, while in the dark brown shirt at the right, they disappear, and the light-colored cross shape emerges. T-shirts by Lassie Wittman.

3-10. Fabrics with insistent patterns in black and white have been skillfully employed in this fascinating composition that is ambiguous, yet ordered. Wall hanging designed and made by Mary Hanson.

3-11. This stunning machine-sewn wall quilt was designed and made by Donna Prichard. The strip patchwork technique could be employed to produce similar designs.

work, "But I'm not creative, I can't do anything original." My reply to this is, first of all, that originality is not the preeminent attribute of the artist. A conscious striving for originality often tends to result in a lack of authenticity, that quality which commands our respect and admiration for any work of art, be it ever so humble.

Anything done expertly, with love and care, is done in the manner of the artist, and artists can grow, just like the proverbial little acorn. Classes in design can be very helpful, provided the right teacher can be found. Courses in art appreciation are also very useful, for they help the student to understand what he or she is looking at. They can provide a vocabulary that develops awareness of good things and how they are made. Never forget that without words we could not think; language not only communicates our thoughts, but in turn expands our capacity to think.

Artistic creation is a kind of dialogue between the doing hand and the perceptive mind and brings into play the full range of our capacities, which is the reason we find such activity so deeply satisfying.

If you really cannot resist working with materials and love to make things, there is surely something of the artist in you, and, if you care to, you can help that artist to grow.

When you bring an armload of art books home from the library, please do more than look at the pretty pictures. Often there are a few observations in the text worth noting; and pay attention to painting and the so-called fine arts, as well as to your favored fiber arts. These things have received the devoted attention of scores of knowledgeable critics and art lovers, and reading what some of these observers have said can help you to learn what good design is all about. Develop the habit of trying to put into words your own responses to the works of art and craft that you encounter. Merely looking at something and liking it or not liking it will never teach you anything.

As you come to understand something about good art and acquire a vocabulary with which to think and talk about it, you will gain confidence in your own judgment, which in turn will generate the climate in which your talents can blossom. For your first effort, select a worthy model to emulate, adapting it to your chosen medium. Many a renowned painter learned his craft by copying masterworks in the museums, and you can learn some valuable lessons by attempting your own version of a fine design.

A great diversity of interesting patterns and designs that can be made by the strip-patchwork technique can be found in architectural decoration, graphic design, mosaics, tapestries, pottery, quilts, Oriental carpets, American Indian painting and basketry, Navajo weaving, ethnic embroidery, mathematical designs, and even in patterns for crochet and knitting.

Useful aids in planning your own designs are $1/8$-inch graph paper, tracing paper, and colored pens and pencils. Fat felt markers can be used to make striped bands for quick experiments, or designs can be tested by cutting and pasting strips of colored paper. A file or notebook for ideas, clippings, and color combinations can be invaluable as a source of inspiration, as well as a resource for problem solving.

When you have developed a design that appeals to you or suits your purpose, sketch it on graph paper and divide it into parallel segments to see whether it might lend itself to the sewn-strips technique.

If you're ready to start designing, the following information will organize your work. There are certain calculations you will have to make beforehand. You will need to know how much fabric is required in each color and how many segments will be needed altogether. These guidelines will show you how to figure this out beforehand, so that once you are ready to sit down and begin, your work will be flowing and uninterrupted. There is nothing quite so annoying as finding out that you don't have enough of a particular fabric, just when you need it.

Since many fabrics come in 45-inch widths, we will assume in this sample that you will be using 45-inch strips. Also, we will assume in this case that your motif consists of two or more differing segments:

Step 1. Draw the motif at the required size on graph paper.

Step 2. Draw the lines through the motif to divide it into its components, or segments.

Step 3. Trace each segment separately, adding seam allowances on all sides, and indicate on each tracing the colors to be used.

Step 4. Tack the single segment on a large sheet of paper. Extend the line or lines depicting the strips in the strip-band needed to make that segment and the lines denoting the top and the bottom of the band. Remove the segment pattern and connect the lines showing the strips. Label each strip with the appropriate color. Also, write in the width of each strip, adding seam allowances where necessary. (Note that for the ¼-inch seams, ½ inch will be added for all the strips except those at the top and bottom of the strip-band, since the seam allowance at the top and bottom were added in tracing each segment. Do the same for each segment in the motif. You now have a list of the colors and widths needed to make each strip-band.

Step 5. Determine how many segments of each kind can be cut from the strip-band by dividing the length of the strip-band by the width of the segment. For example, if each segment is 1½ inches wide, you can cut thirty segments altogether. To find the number of diagonal segments that can be cut from each band, draw a line vertical to the base of the segment to depict the end of the strip-band. Label this line AD, as shown in Figure 3–12. Label the width of the segment BC. Subtract the distance AB from the total length of the strip-band, and divide the result by the width of the segments BC to find the number of segments that can be cut from each band.

Step 6. Decide how many motifs will be needed altogether for your project, and list the number of segments of each kind that will be needed. For example:

Segment	Quantity Needed
Segment A	60
Segment B	60
Segment C	30

You now know how many of each strip-band you will need, if thirty segments can be cut from each band.

Strip-Band	Quantity Needed
Strip-Band A	2
Strip-Band B	2
Strip-Band C	1

Step 7. To determine how much fabric in each color you will need, list the colors and widths of the strips needed for each strip-band:

Strip-Band A	Green	1½ inches
	Yellow	1 inch
	Red	1½ inches
Strip-Band B	Yellow	1 inch
	Red	2 inches
	Green	1 inch

Step 8. List each color separately, make a tally, and base your yardage on this.

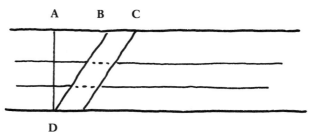

3–12. How to find the number of diagonal segments that can be cut from a strip-band.

4

STRIP PATCHWORK FOR QUILTS

For the making of machine-sewn patchwork quilt tops, the strip patchwork technique offers advantages in speed, convenience, and precision. With a little practice, you can easily develop skill in making bands of parallel strips, the seams of which match precisely when cut and sewn again.

Of course, the idea of joining strips into bands to be cut and sewn again is certainly not new to the experienced quilt maker, and many fine quilts, old and new, combine hand-sewn and machine-sewn elements. The familiar Nine Patch, Roman Stripe, and Rail Fence, as well as the Spider Web and other so-called "string quilts," are some that come to mind. If you are new to quilt making and plan to make a machine-sewn quilt top for the first time, you may wish to familiarize yourself with some of these old traditional patterns before deciding upon a design. In the Bibliography are listed some excellent books on quilt making that show these old patterns, as well as many others that can be made with sewn strips. When looking for a particular pattern, do not count on the name alone to identify it, since many quilt blocks have various names. Sometimes the name of a quilt design may refer to the method of making it, rather than to the design of the block itself.

(The term "string quilt" was originally used to designate patterns made from long, narrow scraps of miscellaneous lengths and widths. These were often sewn to a backing of cloth or paper (the latter being torn away later), and cut in the shapes desired. You will often see a quilt labeled "string quilt" which has long bands in it composed of many short narrow strips. You may also find the traditional Spider Web pattern labeled "The String Quilt" because it is a well-known application of the string method. However, the way this old pattern is put together has no relationship to the Spider Web block shown in Figure 4–9, which is an adaptation by the author to the strip patchwork technique.)

Other traditional patterns that can be made of narrow strips are the Roman Stripe, in which short narrow strips in random colors are sewn to make squares, which are then set together with the stripes alternating horizontally and vertically. In the Rail Fence, blocks of stripes are set together similarly, but there is a set order of colors in the stripes, which produces the distinctive overall pattern. The Nine Patch, usually composed of nine equal squares set together in a symmetrical pattern, can also be made of unlike pieces. (See Figure 4–15.) All can be made of segments cut from bands of three strips each.

4-1. A simple block that can be made with one strip-band is the mitered square.

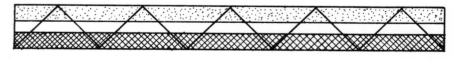

4-2. Making the strip-band in Figure 4-1.

There are a number of attractive patterns that are simple to plan, as well as to sew, that can be made from the segments or pieces cut from a single strip-band alone. One of the simplest of these is the mitered square shown in Figure 4-1, which is the basis of a number of variations. To make this three strips of equal width are sewn together, and the resulting band is cut as shown in Figure 4-2. The strips may be of any width. Those used in the example are each 2 inches wide and make a block about 8 inches square when four of the triangular pieces are sewn together.

A similar pattern could be made using four

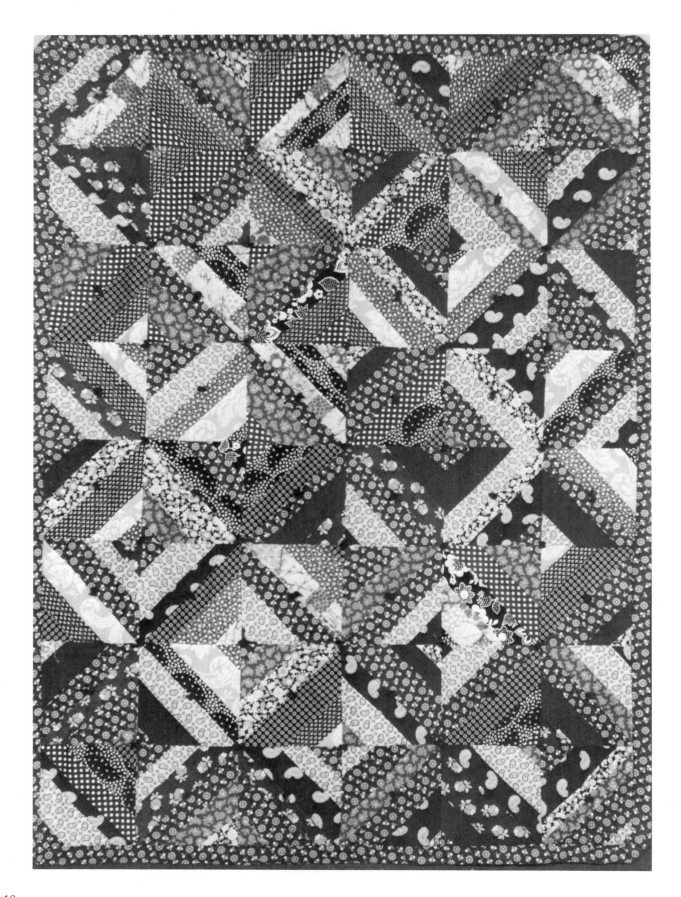

48

colors, instead of three. The colors would alternate when put together, instead of forming a frame around the center, as in Figure 4–1. A color for this center strip that would contrast strongly in value with the adjacent strips should not be selected, unless you wish to emphasize the frame shape. The colors used in the sample were plain medium brown, a print in two tones of rose, and one in brown, rose, black, and white on light gray.

When marking these triangles on the band for cutting, take care to cut an equal number of each triangle. If the sewn strip-band yields an uneven number of triangular pieces, be sure to place the pattern on alternate bands in such a way that the two bands yield an equal number of each. Four triangular pieces are needed to make one block.

In the Treasure Box afghan shown in Figure 4–3 the bands were cut as in the previous example. This quilt can easily be made in any size. Several different strip-bands were made, with strips varying in width and the pieces arranged to make a seemingly random, yet artful, pattern. The dimensions are 48 by 65 inches. Three and one-half yards of 45-inch fabric were needed to make the backing, which was turned over the front to finish the edge. For the strip-bands, assorted pieces of ½ or ¼ yard (totaling 3½ yards) were torn into strips 2, 2½, and 3 inches wide, making bands 6½ inches wide.

Remnants of random colors and random narrow widths could be used to make similar blocks, which could be alternated with squares or diagonal half squares of plain materials in various colors.

Another very effective pattern that is made from pieces cut from a single strip-band is the one shown in Figure 4–4. It consists of alternating dark and light octagons. Figure 4–5 shows how the band first is cut into squares and then each is cut into four triangular pieces. Eight of these triangular pieces are needed to make each block. They are sorted so that four pieces with dark-colored strips are used in one block, and four with the light-colored strips are

used in the other. The triangles with the upright stripes can be arranged as desired; experiment to see what can happen. For maximum effectiveness the light and dark values of the colors you select should be distributed as in the example.

I decided it was best to join the triangles with horizontal stripes to those with vertical stripes, as shown in Figure 4–6, and then sew the squares together. When joining the blocks, place one over the other so that the center seams line up; use a ruler to mark the seamline with pins. The seam allowance may appear uneven, but the seams will be straight.

To make the Octagon pattern just as it is shown in Figure 4–4 use the following colors and widths for the strip-band:

Color	Width
Black	2½ inches
Violet	1 inch
Rose print	2 inches
Black print	2 inches
Plain rose	1 inch
Ecru dotted	2½ inches

When sewn together, these make a band 8½ inches wide, which, when cut, sorted, and assembled will make blocks about 10 inches square. The finished blocks measure 9½ inches. Five squares can be cut from a strip-band of 45-inch fabric, and eight of the triangular pieces are needed to make each block. Thus, one strip-band yields two and one-half blocks. To make the hanging shown, nine blocks were used, requiring four strip-bands. Four large triangles of plain color were sewn to the sides to make the larger square. The bands of black at the edges are 2 inches wide, with a ½-inch strip of violet separating it from the background of deep rose. The light-colored octagon block left over could be used to make a pillow, or a super-size pot holder or mat.

To use this design for a quilt or coverlet an uneven number of blocks running across horizontally and vertically should be used. A top measuring about 47 by 85 inches (five blocks across and nine down, or forty-five in all) would require eighteen strip-bands. Using the guide given in Chapter 3 for finding total yardage required for an original project should enable you to plan a quilt in whatever dimensions are needed.

4–3. To make the Treasure Box afghan bands of three strips were cut as shown in Figure 4–2, but, because many different strip-bands were used, the result is quite different. Afghan made by Liz McCord.

4-4. This design of dark and light octagons is cut from one strip-band. Wall hanging by the author.

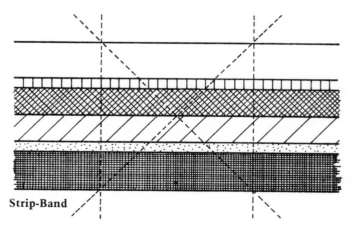

Strip-Band

4-5. Making the octagon pattern shown in Figure 4-4.

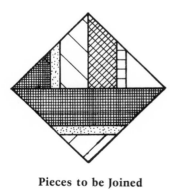

Pieces to be Joined

4-6. When making the block, join these pieces first.

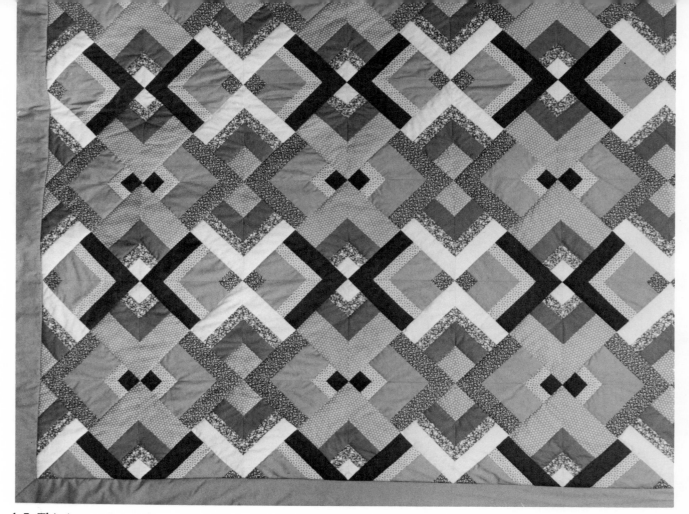

4–7. This interesting quilt is made of pieces cut from two different strip-bands. Quilt designed and made by Lassie Wittman.

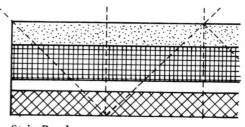

Strip-Band a

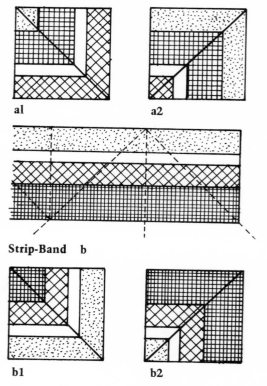

Figure 4–7 shows an interesting quilt pattern made of triangular pieces cut from two different strip-bands. The colors—browns, beiges, rust, orange, and black—make a striking pattern. Figure 4–8 shows how the strip-bands were cut. Can you figure out how the pieces were put together? They can be assembled in various other ways, and it would be a good idea to make the two strip-bands of colored paper, cut them as shown, and experiment with various arrangements before proceeding to make a similar quilt.

4–8. Making and cutting the strip-bands for the quilt in Figure 4–7.

Still another way of using only one strip-band to make a block is shown in Figure 4–9, an example of the Spider Web pattern. Figure 4–10 shows how the segments are arranged on the band for cutting.

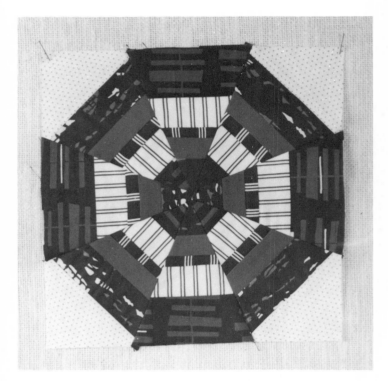

4–9. A block for the Spider Web pattern can be made with one strip-band. Sample designed and made by Mary Hanson.

To make a pattern for the Spider Web block fold a square of paper the size of the block you want twice diagonally. Fold it again, to make eight layers. Fold once more, as shown in Figure 4–11, and mark point X. Open up the square, and draw lines across the corners from these points. Make templates for one side piece and one corner piece of the pattern, as shown in Figure 4–10, adding ¼-inch seam allowances on all sides. You will need to experiment with colored stripes drawn on paper to work out your color plan and a good dark and light pattern.

Shown in Figure 4–12 is a handsome example of the Lone Star pattern done in strip patchwork. The design was ingeniously devised in that it requires only three wide strip-bands to make the pattern. Figure 4–13 shows one diamond-shaped section of the large star. The star consists of eight diamonds. Each diamond is comprised of seven segments cut from bands of seven strips. Segments # 1, # 4, and # 7 in the diamond are made with Strip-Band # 1; Segments # 2 and # 5 are made with # 2; and Segments # 3 and # 6 with # 3. All the pieces that make up the quilt top were sewn together by machine. The border, made of the same segments that comprise the star, is especially pleasing, and the hand-quilting in the corners makes this piece a classic.

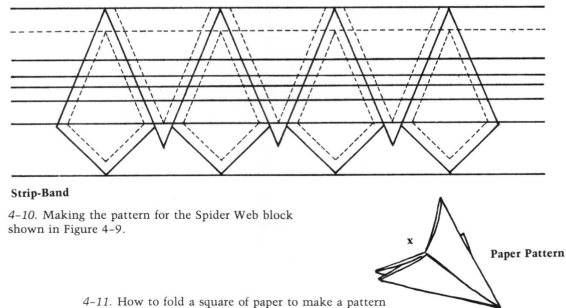

Strip-Band

4–10. Making the pattern for the Spider Web block shown in Figure 4–9.

x

Paper Pattern

4–11. How to fold a square of paper to make a pattern for the Spider Web block.

4–12. This Lone Star pattern is made with three different strip-bands. Quilt designed and made by Joanne Haldeman.

4–13. Making and combining the segments in the Lone Star quilt in Figure 4–12.

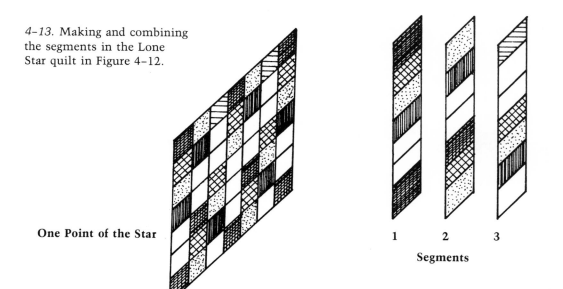

One Point of the Star

1   2   3

Segments

4-14. In this lively design, variations on the Nine Patch block are combined with chevron borders. Quilt by Joanne Haldeman.

A favorite pattern among quilt makers is the Nine Patch. There is a definite advantage to making the Nine Patch pattern from bands of strips of equal width. The patterns can be regular or random and can be used in an almost infinite number of ways. In the quilt shown in Figure 4–14, small Nine Patch blocks in random colors are put together with squares of plain dark blue to make larger blocks of nine, and these are alternated with large squares of plain dark blue to make the center. This arrangement is sometimes called Cat in the Corner. Other small Nine Patch blocks in the outer borders are made with the colors in a regular order. They create an interesting pattern of dark and light between the bands of chevrons.

This popular variation of the Nine Patch shown in Figure 4–15 is made with strip-bands that have a center strip wider than those at the edges. The center segment is also cut wider than those at the sides, so that the center piece in the block is a square, and there are four smaller squares in the corners. For all its simplicity, this pattern is very pleasing. Notice how the colors have been handled in the blocks around the edges, creating a border effect. To achieve this result, it is necessary to depict the coverlet in its entirety on paper, and then count the number of each kind of segment needed.

The Double Irish Chain, shown in Figure 4–16 could be thought of as an elaboration of the Nine Patch, being composed of blocks made from five strips of equal width sewn together instead of only three and set alternately with blocks having one small square in each corner, as shown in Figure 4–17.

If you plan to make a coverlet based on the Nine Patch block or the Double Irish Chain, draw a few blocks on graph paper to get an idea of the repeat and decide how many blocks you will need for the size of quilt you plan to make.

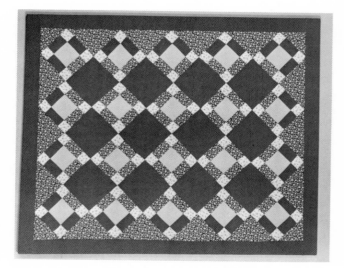

4-15. An attractive variation of the Nine Patch pattern. Quilt made by Liz McCord.

4-16. The Double Irish Chain pattern.

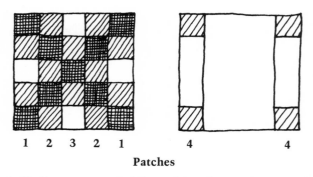

1   2   3   2   1   4   4

Patches

4-17. Segments needed for making the Double Irish Chain.

Try to visualize how you want it to appear on the bed and decide whether to cover the entire surface or to contain the guilt within wide borders of plain fabric, as in some of the wonderful Amish quilts. When you have decided on the size of the small squares needed to make the blocks, make a pattern for each segment and mark it with the colors to be used. Follow the directions in Chapter 3 for organizing your work.

To determine how much you need of each color, again make a list, as follows:

Strip-Band	Color	Width
Strip-Band # 1	Black	3 inches
	Black	3 inches
	Red	3 inches
	Red	3 inches
	White	3 inches
Strip-Band # 2	Black	3 inches
	Black	3 inches
	Red	3 inches
	Red	3 inches

etc.

Be sure to label each operation as you go. If making calculations of this sort is confusing to you, I suggest that you make one sample of each strip-band required, cutting the segments and making up as many blocks as can be made from these bands. Then use this information to determine the amounts of material needed for the quilt you want to make.

The name Log Cabin is given to several patterns made of narrow strips. Most often these are joined to make square blocks divided diagonally into darker and lighter colors, creating various patterns depending on how they are set together. Similar blocks made by the strip technique can also be set in these well-known traditional patterns. (See bibliography.)

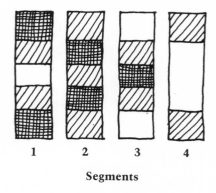

1   2   3   4

Segments

A different version of the Log Cabin pattern known as Courthouse Steps is shown in Figure 4–18. It was one of my first experiments with the strip technique.

In the example the finished segments are only ½ inch wide, creating a rich surface that has the appearance of quilting. I cannot fathom why it did not occur to me to turn alternate blocks when assembling, unless it was just that my mind was so focused upon the continuous bands of the Seminoles I overlooked other considerations. Done this way, it was necessary to make two different sets of blocks in order not to have long stripes of the same color running the length of the piece. This disadvantage has been corrected in Figure 4–19. This design was used to make a coverlet of 7-inch blocks. In this revised design only one set of bands needs to be made, and by alternately turning the blocks, attractive patterns in the light areas are created.

To make this into a quilt or coverlet to cover an area of 56 by 63 inches, seventy-two 7-inch blocks are needed—eight across and nine down. For a larger piece, increase the number of blocks or add a border of plain fabric, with perhaps an additional outer border of 1-inch strips vertical to the edge. You will need three light colors, three dark colors, and a fourth dark color for the plain segments in the centers. Purchase 45-inch fabric in the following amounts: 30 inches of each light color; 12 inches of one dark color, 24 inches of the second dark color, and one yard of the third; 24 inches of the fourth dark color.

The total amount of material required is $5\frac{1}{6}$ yards for the seventy-two blocks. Additional fabric will be needed for borders.

Label the light colors with letters, and the dark colors with numbers and make a list as follows:

Strip-Band	Color	Width
Strip-Band # 1	1	1½ inches
	x	3½ inches
	z	3½ inches
Strip-Band # 2	2	3½ inches
	y	2½ inches
	y	2½ inches
Strip-Band # 3	3	5½ inches
	x	1½ inches
	z	1½ inches

Once you've done the preliminary figuring out, you're ready to do the actual sewing. The work consists of three basic steps:

Step 1. Join strips to make the three strip-bands, each with the dark colors in the center. After pressing, mark and cut each strip-band into 1½-inch segments.

Step 2. Arrange the segments in the order you desire, and sew them together into blocks. The illustration shows one way of arranging the segments, but feel free to come up with your own arrangement. Press the seams in one direction.

Step 3. Join the blocks, turning them alternately so that the seams run vertically and horizontally in adjacent blocks.

Segments 1 inch wide (when finished) look more like the traditional Log Cabin pattern than do wider ones and make a more elegant surface. Also, should you wish to enlarge the size of the blocks, it would be simplest to use 1-inch segments and to increase the number of them. To do this draw a diagram of the block you plan to make on graph paper. Label the light colors with letters and the dark colors with numbers. Make a list of the strips needed for each strip-band, as for instance for a 9-inch block:

Strip-Band	Color	Width
Strip-Band # 1	w	4½ inches
	1	1½ inches
	z	4½ inches
Strip-Band # 2	x	3½ inches
	2	3½ inches
	y	3½ inches
Strip-Band # 3	y	2½ inches
	3	5½ inches
	x	2½ inches
Strip-Band # 4	z	1½ inches
	4	7½ inches
	w	1½ inches

You can now determine how much of each color you will need by counting the number of segments of each kind in the diagram you have drawn and dividing by the number of segments that can be cut from one strip-band.

4-18. A variation of the Log Cabin block, known as Courthouse Steps, made in the strip technique. Quilt made by the author.

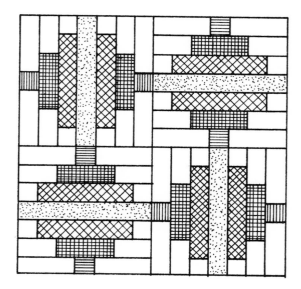

Block

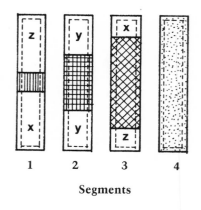

Segments

4-19. Turning alternate blocks when assembling the Courthouse Steps pattern improves the design, and requires only one set of strip-bands.

4-20. A section of a Log Cabin pattern, adapted to the strip technique. Quilt made by the author.

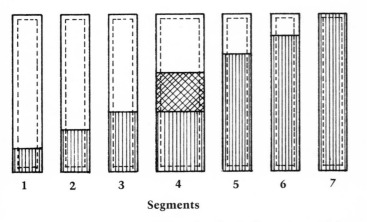

1   2   3   4   5   6   7

Segments

4-21. Segments needed to make the quilt in Figure 4-20.

Another of my initial experiments with the Log Cabin pattern is shown in Figure 4-20. Although somewhat hard to perceive in a black-and-white photograph, the pattern is lively and pleasing and creates a windmill pattern. Here again I sewed the blocks together with all the seams running vertically, which necessitated the use of different colors in the long single-colored strips. What I like about this block is its size, which is 8 inches square, and the 2-inch red square in the center. Figure 4-21 shows how a similar block can be made.

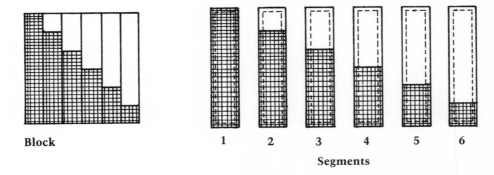

Block   1   2   3   4   5   6

Segments

4-22. The basic plan for making Log Cabin blocks.

The basic plan for making Log Cabin blocks is shown in Figure 4-22. The segments can be any length desired, and the number of segments can be increased to enlarge the blocks. When four blocks are sewn together, a square of one color (the color used for the smaller portion of Segment # 6) is formed where they meet in the center. A way to emphasize this square is to use a contrasting bright color for the small portion in Segment # 6; or, for a different effect, two colors can be used, as shown in Figure 4-23. Still another way of varying the basic block is shown in Figure 4-24.

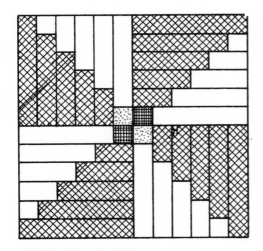

Block

4-23. By using two different colors for the bottom strip in Segment # 6, the square formed at the center of four blocks set together can be varied.

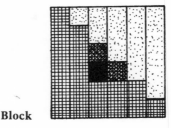

Block

4-24. Another variation of the Log Cabin block.

The example shown in Figure 4–25 is a block often seen in more contemporary Seminole pattern-bands. The Seminoles do not generally use all-over designs, although some of the patches, such as this one, are adaptable for use as quilt blocks. This one can be put together with diagonal half-squares, as shown, or with the corners of the dark half-squares touching each other and the corners of the light half-squares touching. The blocks could also be alternated with squares of plain fabric. For the most pleasing effect, care needs to be taken in juxtaposing colors and values, and it would be best to make rough sketches of various possibilities before assembling the blocks. The three segments needed to make this block are shown in Figure 4–26.

The Medallion quilt shown in Figure 4–27 consists of several motifs typical of contemporary Seminole patterns. Predominantly orange, rust, and bright green, with white, yellow, black, brown, and olive green, the colors are brilliant and intense; the yellow-to-orange shading around the center square appears to glow. The black-and-white photograph reveals a fine handling of dark and light values in the border patterns.

The framed quilt provides a perfect opportunity to employ a variety of border patterns, and could be made into a sampler of strip-sewn bands. It would also be an ideal way to display a treasured piece of handwork, such as a single large block appliquéd with a traditional floral pattern in curving lines and shapes and hand quilted. The center could be a piece of stitchery commemorating a special family event, or an especially choice printed fabric embellished with trapunto or stitchery. Still another possibility would be an original motif done in the strip technique.

4–25. A quilt design based on a square patch often seen in Seminole pattern-bands. Quilt made by Kay Kelly.

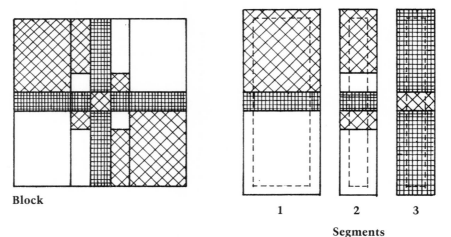

Block

1 **2** **3**

Segments

4–26. Segments needed to make the block in Figure 4–25.

4-27. The Medallion quilt provides a fitting opportunity to use an array of Seminole pattern-bands. Quilt made by Joanne Haldeman.

4-28. A four-pointed star with a traditional look can be made with segments cut from four different strip-bands. Sample designed by the author and sewn by Barbara Rickey.

Block

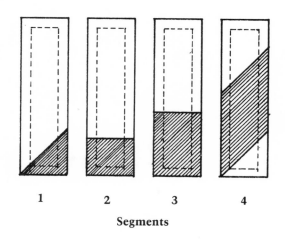

1   2   3   4

Segments

4-29. Segments needed to make the block in Figure 4-28.

Quilt books contain many delightful examples of framed quilts. When looking through some of them for ideas, pay attention to the relative proportions of the various borders. Notice also the treatment of the corners.

The small sample shown in Figure 4–28 is made of navy blue and white sprigged calico on a background of ecru cotton with tiny navy blue dots, to give a traditional look. Four of each segment, cut from four different strip-bands, are needed to make the pattern in each block Sixteen segments make up each block, excluding the plain segments on the sides. The block is 7½ inches square when finished. To make the sample approximately ³/₈ yard of fabric is needed in Color A (the background fabric) and about ¹/₆ yard is needed in Color B (the motif). Make a list of each color needed in the strip-band and the widths of each:

Strip-Band		Color	Width
Strip-Band # 1	(36 inches long)	Color A	3¼ inches
		Color B	1¹/₈ inches
Strip-Band # 2	(20 inches long)	Color A	2¾ inches
		Color B	1¼ inches
Strip-Band # 3	(20 inches long)	Color A	3½ inches
		Color B	2 inches
Strip-Band # 4	(36 inches long)	Color A	1⁵/₈ inches
		Color B	2¹/₈ inches
		Color A	1¹/₈ inches

Cut sixteen segments from each strip, reversing the pattern after cutting eight, to make the pattern, as shown in Figure 4–29. For the plain strips at the sides, tear a strip of Color A 20 inches long and 4½ inches wide and cut it into sixteen 1¼-inch segments.

Join the segments across into patches of eight, following the illustration, then join with the other group of eight to make the design shown.

To make a quilt top 60 by 75 inches (eighty blocks) ten strip-bands for Segments # 2 and # 3 and fourteen strip-bands for Segments # 1 and # 4 are needed.

Anyone who is fascinated by tessellations will find that many such patterns can be made with sewn bands of fabric. The striking motif, shown in Figure 4–30, known as Fly Foot or Crazy Ann, requires only one strip-band, the segments of which are reversed to make the second half of each unit within the block. Made in antique style calico prints, it looks charmingly old-fashioned; or, made in rich, deep tones of plain heavy cotton or drapery fabric in large scale, it would make a smart contemporary bedspread or couch cover. The block is composed of four units consisting of two segments each (in other words, eight segments), and is 8 inches square when finished.

To make a sample of four blocks ⅓ yard of background fabric and about ¹/₆ yard of the motif fabric are needed.

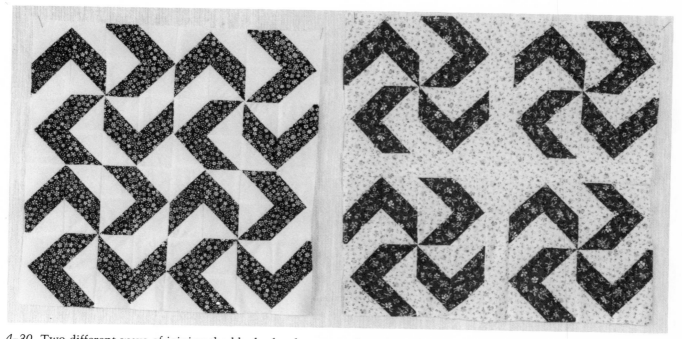

4–30. Two different ways of joining the blocks for the pattern known as Fly Foot or Crazy Ann.

To cut the thirty-two segments required three strip-bands are needed. The center strips should be $1^7/_8$ inches wide, and the ones on each side 2 inches wide. From one of these bands, mark and cut eleven segments; reverse the pattern to cut eleven from the second. The ten remaining segments needed can be cut from the third band.

To make the pattern for the segment, draw a rectangle 2 by 4 inches, and add ¼-inch seam allowances on all sides. Draw the lines indicating the center strip on both sides of the pattern, or make a second pattern for cutting the reverse of the segment.

Sort the segments into lots of two and sew them together to form the basic chevron units. After pressing the seams, arrange them as shown in Figure 4–31. When sewing the four pieces together, take care to pin the edges to be joined, as it is quite easy to sew the wrong edges together. When four units have been joined to make the block, all four sides should be alike, and the blocks can be sewn together without danger of joining the wrong edges.

If you have admired various hexagon patterns, but have been deterred from attempting to make one by the thought of the long hours of hand sewing involved in joining these shapes, which must be basted over paper and whipped together by hand, you will be pleased to learn that some hexagon patterns can be made with your faithful sewing machine and the strip technique. See Figures 4–32 and 4–33. Different patterns can be produced by varying the arrangement of the colors.

Only one segment pattern is needed to cut the pieces required, and it is easy to see the pattern developing as you assemble it. Two segments of a color are joined to make each hexagon, and the sixteen hexagons can be arranged to make the all-over pattern.

Figure 4–34 shows how four colors can be used to make a pattern with a solid-color six-pointed star between the clusters of hexagons in alternating colors. To make a quilt top about 72 inches by 63 inches, of 6-inch hexagons, you will need a total of 7⅓ yards of fabric in the following amounts: 1⅔ yards each of Colors # 1 and # 2, ⅔ yard of Color # 3, and 3⅓ yards of Color # 4.

This amount of material will make nine groups of sixteen hexagons, which, of course, will have to be arranged to fit a rectangular space. You may want to work out some way to use plain segments at the edges to set off the clusters of hexagons. You will need the following widths in each color to make the strip-bands:

Strip-Band	Colors	Width	Number of Strips
# 1	# 1	$5^3/_8$ inches	10
	# 4	$3^1/_8$ inches	10
# 2	# 2	$5^3/_8$ inches	10
	# 4	$3^1/_8$ inches	10
# 3	# 3	$5^3/_8$ inches	4
	# 4	$3^1/_8$ inches	4
# 4	# 4	$5^3/_8$ inches	4

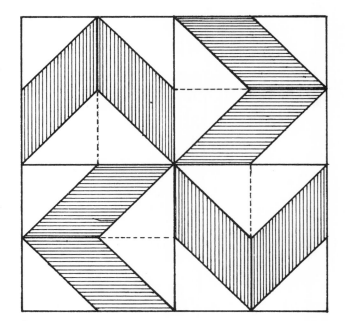

Segment

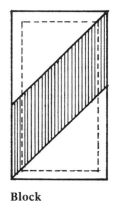

Block

4–31. One segment pattern and its mirror image are needed to make the pattern in Figure 4–30.

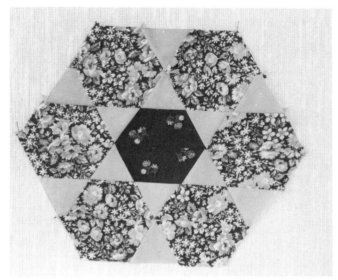

4-32. The ever-popular Hexagon pattern can be made with the strip technique. The sections of sixteen hexagons shown can be sewn to each other to form clusters of seven hexagons in alternating colors. Sample made by Barbara Rickey and designed by the author.

To make a template for the segment, draw a parallelogram with sides 6 inches and 3 inches, having two angles of 60 degrees. To mark it with the line denoting the color change place it as shown in Figure 4-34 and draw a line from the center point of the left-hand side to the opposite lower corner. Add ¼-inch seams on all sides.

4-33. A rosette of seven hexagons, which would make a charming pillow top, can be made of fourteen segments, by ripping off the small triangles from four of the outer segments and sewing two of them back on, as needed. Example made by Barbara Rickey.

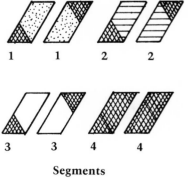

Segments

Section

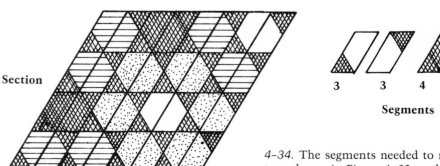

4-34. The segments needed to make the hexagon pattern shown in Figure 4-32, and how they are sewn together.

65

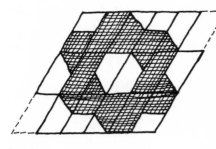

Section

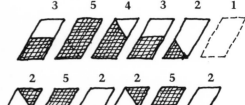

Segments

4-35. To make the traditional Honeycomb pattern of hexagons two kinds of strip-bands are needed, and the segments cut from them would be combined as shown.

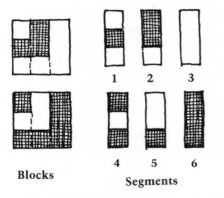

Blocks   **Segments**

4-36. Blocks made from the segments shown can be used to create tessellations.

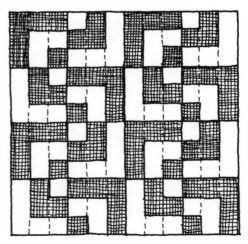

Tessellated Patterns

An examination of the traditional Honeycomb pattern revealed that the number of differing segments required would make it a relatively complicated pattern to create in strip patchwork. However, it is indeed possible to do, and the dedicated quilt buff who cherishes a special fondness for hexagons may enjoy pursuing this entertaining project. Shown in Figure 4-35 is a hint that may help you tackle it.

As you can see, three different segments are needed to make this pattern. You would need to make a color sketch of the pattern desired, and figure out how many of each kind and color of segment would be required to make it.

To experiment with the pattern shown in Figure 4-35, you might like to make a pillow top, adding strips of the background color where needed, and trimming it to make the hexagon shape.

4-37. Two ways of arranging the blocks shown in Figure 4-36.

66

4–38. A variation of the Tulip pattern, designed to fit a square. Sample made by the author.

Other kinds of tessellated patterns are suggested by Figures 4–36 and 4–37. The six segments in Figure 4–36, which make two blocks that are the reverse of each other, can be arranged in a variety of ways.

In the example shown in Figure 4–38, a variation of the charming old Tulip pattern has been made to fit a square. Intended for a pillow top, it is made of black wool, with lovely shades of red, rose, and soft green. The proportions of the original block have been observed in Figure 4–39, and can easily be adapted to various sizes of quilt tops. The number of blocks needed will depend upon the size quilt you plan to make, how large you make the blocks, and whether you plan to have the blocks overhang the top of the bed just slightly, with plain fabric and borders to finish it, or whether you use the blocks to cover the entire surface of the quilt.

4–39. The block for the traditional Tulip pattern shown in Figure 4–38 and the segments needed for making it.

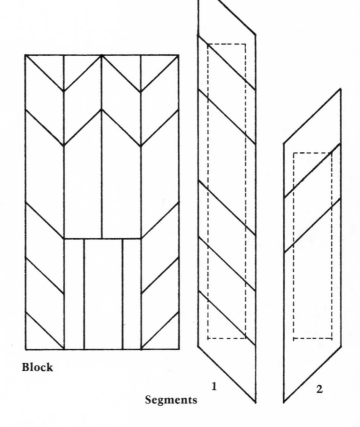

Block

Segments

1

2

This block is usually alternated with plain blocks of the background material, which could be of unbleached muslin.

To make the templates needed for your quilt, proceed as follows:

Step 1. Make a tracing of the Tulip block in Figure 4–39 and on it draw lines midway through the vertical segments. Draw horizontal lines the same distance apart to make a grid of squares.

Step 2. Draw a rectangle in the desired size, mark it with a grid to correspond to the tracing, and draw the diagonal lines to make a full-size drawing of your block. Trace Segments #1 and #2 separately, and add ¼ inch for seams on all sides. Trace the lines that separate the colors on both sides of the segments, and label each one.

To find how many of each segment are required, you will need to make a thumbnail sketch of your quilt, and count them. (See directions given in Chapter 3 for determining total fabric needed.)

The widths of the strips needed to make blocks 6 inches by 12 inches are listed below. The colors designated are merely for convenience, and are listed in order from the bottom to the top of the band, since this is the order in which they are sewn.

Strip-Band	Color	Width
Strip-Band #1	Natural	1³/₈ inches
	Green	1⁵/₈ inches
	Natural	1⁵/₈ inches
	Red	2⁵/₈ inches
	Rose	1⁵/₈ inches
	Natural	1³/₈ inches
Strip-Band #2	Red	3³/₄ inches
	Rose	1⁵/₈ inches
	Natural	1³/₈ inches

Sew the strips together in the order given, for each strip-band, and press the seams toward the bottom of the band. Lay Pattern #1 on the wider band so that the lines coincide with the proper colors. (Don't forget to reverse the template to cut the segments from alternate bands, to make both sides of the flower.) Trace and cut the segments. Using Pattern #2, cut the segments from the narrower bands. (Ten of the longer segments can be cut from one 45-inch strip-band and eleven of the shorter ones.)

To make the striped bands for the stems you will need:

Color	Width
Natural	1¼ inches
Green	2 inches
Natural	1¼ inches

Sew these strips together with the green strip in the center; press and cut into 5-inch pieces.

To assemble the block sew the two shorter segments together according to the illustration, and sew the 5-inch piece for the stem to the lower edge of this piece after trimming off the point. Then sew the two longer segments to each side.

In the original coverlet from which this pattern was taken, the block appears to have been about 7 inches by 14 inches, which would be a good size for making a king-size bedspread. An attractive and appropriate border for this would be one of the various chevron borders shown at the end of this chapter. If you want to make the block in a size other than that for which directions are given, here are the general directions for planning a project using long diagonal segments:

Step 1. Mark a large, plain sheet of paper with a 45-degree diagonal at one end, as shown in Figure 4–40. Tack your segment pattern in place along this line, and draw line DC. Lay a ruler across the segment and draw the lines denoting the colored strips onto the paper; label these with the colors you plan to use. Remove the pattern and complete the lines if necessary.

Step 2. Measure each of the labeled strips and write this measurement opposite the color. Add the amount needed for seams on each strip, in the following manner: Green, 1⁵/₈ inches plus ½ inch (for 2 seams) equals 2¹/₈ inches. The strips at the top and bottom of the band already include one seam allowance; add ¼ inch only.

Step 3. Make a list of the colors to be used, and write down the widths of the strips needed, according to the directions given in Chapter 3. From this list you can compile the amounts of each color needed for one strip-band.

Step 4. Following the directions given in Chapter 3, make a list of the colors in each strip-band and of the number of strip-bands needed, to determine the total amount of fabric required for your project.

Step 5. To find how many segments can be cut from each strip-band refer again to the large sheet of paper made in Step 1. Mark points A and B, as shown in Figure 4–41, and measure the distance between them. Subtract this amount from the total length of the strip-band. Divide the result by the measurement BC to find the number of segments that can be cut from the band.

The distance BC for the 6- by 12-inch Tulip block was conveniently close to 3 inches, which made it easy to do the necessary arithmetic. Should this number be a troublesome fraction, multiply it by ten, or whatever you estimate to be a reasonable amount, and adjust your guess by approximation. You could simply use a piece of paper long enough to mark off with the segment pattern.

Diagonal segments, such as those used for the Tulip and the Thistle Blossom patterns, tend to curve when sewn together. When pinning them together, lay them straight on a flat surface along the edge of a yardstick or ruler. Place a second ruler along the seamline and place pins in a few places to assure a straight seam. When sewing, treat it as you would any bias seam, stretching it gently to avoid a tight or puckered seam. Occasionally, you may find that one of the segments is crooked for one reason or another. This can usually be corrected by taking the seam in a little deeper where needed.

When all of the segments have been assembled into a block, measure the block and make sure it is square before sewing to the adjoining blocks. If you find it is too wide, do not simply trim it along one or both of its sides, but observe whether some of the segments are wider than others, and take the seams in *very slightly* to adjust the width of the block. (This will make the adjacent segment a trifle narrower, and, therefore, might not be feasible in some cases.) Should the block be wider at one end than the other, you may be able to correct this by tapering the seams at the wider end. Usually a hair's breadth is sufficient. However, if one segment is definitely sewn off the parallel and the adjacent segment is perfect, you may need to rip and adjust accordingly. Check the depth of your seams after making the first block to be sure the blocks will be the right width when finished.

It is not necessary to trim the edges of the blocks if they are slightly uneven at the edges. When joining them, lay a ruler along the seamline, mark it with pins, and draw a line if you wish. Even though the seam allowances may appear to be uneven, the seams will be perfectly straight. Care taken in joining the blocks will save needless trouble and will assure good results.

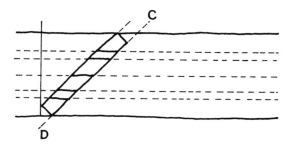

4–40. How to find the widths of the strips needed to make the segments for the Tulip pattern. Line DC, drawn at an angle of 45 degrees to the baseline of the band, shows how the pattern is laid on the strip-band.

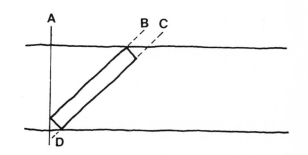

4–41. How to find how many diagonal segments can be cut from each strip-band.

4-42. ''Thistle Blossom'' is a pattern designed by the author to test the practicality of the strip technique. The quilt top was put together by the author's aunt, Ida Koria.

This small coverlet in the pattern I call Thistle Blossom, shown in Figure 4–42, was made to test the practicality of the strip patchwork method and to discover any problems that might arise in the construction. Colors used in the block are rose pink, rose-violet, and medium avocado green, on a sunny light green background. Ten segments, each 1 inch wide, make the 10-inch square. A wide band of plain violet surrounds the two decorative bands that enclose the center. The squares between the patchwork blocks are of print fabric in soft shades of rose and green on a white background. These could be of plain material and could be quilted either by hand or by machine. The blocks could also be used with frames of plain fabric between them.

The proportions of the block are shown in Figure 4–43, and it can be enlarged to make a square of the size you want. To make the quilt, trace each segment full size, add seam allowances, and proceed according to the instructions previously given.

Measurements for making the strip-bands for the 10-inch block are given below:

Strip-Band	Color	Width
Strip-Band # 1	Light Green	$2^5/_8$ inches
	Darker Green	$2^5/_8$ inches
	Violet	$1^7/_8$ inches
	Pink	$1\frac{1}{4}$ inches
	Light Green	$2^5/_8$ inches
Strip-Band # 2	Light Green	4 inches
	Dark Green	$1^5/_8$ inches
	Violet	$1\frac{1}{4}$ inches
	Pink	$1\frac{1}{4}$ inches
	Light Green	3 inches
Strip-Band # 3	Light Green	5 inches
	Dark Green	$^7/_8$ inches
	Pink	$1\frac{1}{4}$ inches
	Light Green	$3^3/_8$ inches
Strip-Band # 4	Light Green	$2^3/_8$ inches
	Dark Green	$1\frac{1}{4}$ inches
	Light Green	$6\frac{1}{4}$ inches

Plain segments for the sides of the blocks should be cut on the bias.

4-43. Diagram of the "Thistle Blossom" pattern. Dimensions of the strips needed for a 10-inch block are given in the directions for making the coverlet.

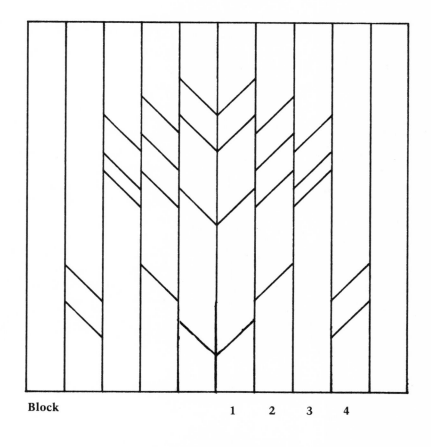

Block   1   2   3   4

Quilt Borders provide a fascinating subject of study and can tell us much about the artistry of the quilt maker. For one design, the simplest edge imaginable can provide the master stroke; in another, the border may be as important as the center in maintaining the integrity of the composition. When browsing through the many wonderful books on fine quilts, study the variety of borders and their relationship to the body of the quilt. Notice whether the border merely defines the edge, adds the final perfect touch, or provides a graceful note of its own. There are some patterns for which any but the plainest edging strip would be a distraction, while there are others that require the support or containment of a border that will reiterate the theme.

The quilts made by the Amish show a profound understanding of the functions of color and proportion, and their knowing ways with borders, deceptively simple to the casual observer, are worthy of careful scrutiny.

The sawtooth border can be used in many different ways, sometimes pointing its teeth in toward the body of the quilt, sometimes turned toward the outer edge, standing out in vividly contrasting values, or providing a subtle demarcation between elements in closely related colors and values. The way in which a border is used is often more telling than the selection of the pattern itself.

If a border is to form the drop at the side and end of the bed cover, take care to consider how it will appear in this position. Corner treatments, too, can be an important asset to the design.

The strip patchwork technique is particularly applicable to the making of borders for quilts. Figure 4-44 illustrates a brick pattern and two ways to use a simple border of blocks.

The borders shown in Figure 4-45 can all be made easily of machine-sewn strips. Diamonds also make attractive borders; see Chapter 2 for directions for horizontal and vertical diamonds.

By cutting down the center of a row of diagonal squares and rearranging the resulting bands, a very pleasing wave pattern can be made, as shown in Figure 4-46.

The ever popular sawtooth border, shown in Figure 4-47a, can be made from a band of two colors. However, using three, as shown, saves fabric, as the dark color is not wasted. More strips can be sewn together, as shown in Figure 4-47b, to save time as well as material.

Segments cut from the strip-band at an oblique angle make the tall, narrow saw teeth, shown in Figure 4-47c.

Chevrons, shown in Figure 4-48a and 4-48b, can be deep or shallow and made of varied colors. Two ways of arranging segments to make chevron borders are shown in Figure 4-48c.

Borders of diagonal stripes lend themselves to endless variations, as shown in Figure 4-49. Colors may be merged or contrasted with the background, or the striped bands can be made of several colors.

Note: To save material when making wide bands of diagonal stripes, join them as shown in Figure 4-50. For the Navajo blanket shown in Chapter 5 I used woolens from old skirts which were mostly about 24 inches long. Had I sewn the strips together to make rectangles, large triangular pieces would have been wasted when cutting the wide bias strips for the bands of chevrons, and I would have run short of material in the needed colors.

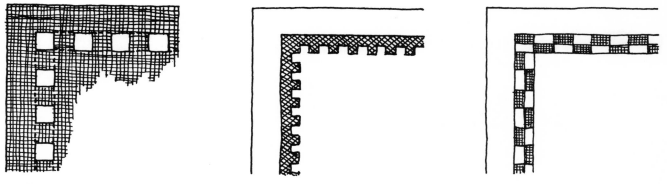

Borders

4-44. A border in the brick pattern, and two ways of using rows of squares in borders.

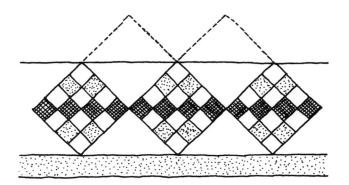

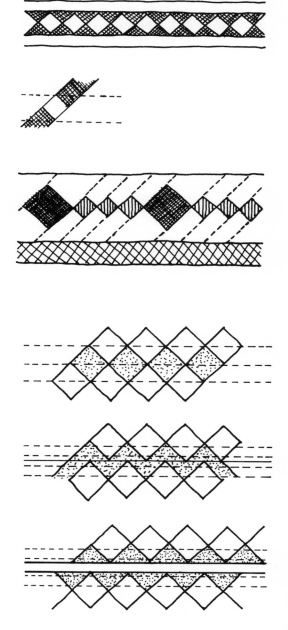

Borders

4-45. Diagonal squares used in quilt borders.

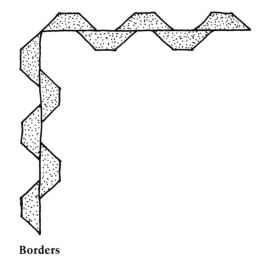

Borders

4-46. One way to make a wave pattern for a border.

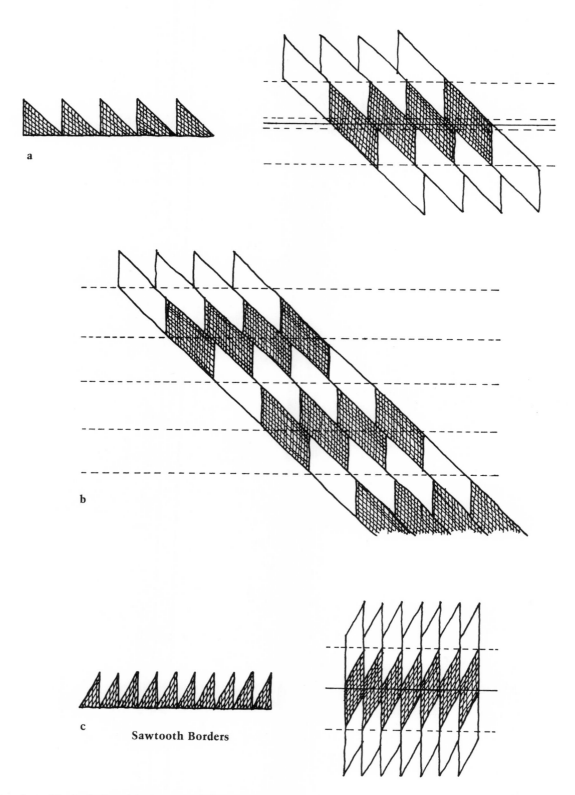

a

b

c

Sawtooth Borders

4-47 *a, b, c.* Method of making sawtooth borders. Figure 47b shows a way to save fabric when making long borders.

74

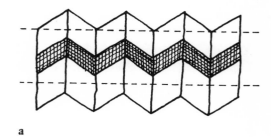
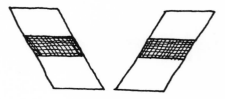

a

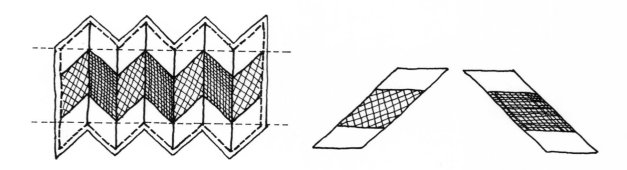

b

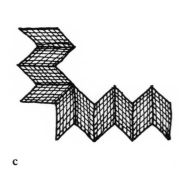

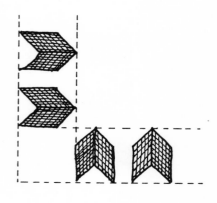

c

Chevron Borders

4-48 a, b, c. Various ways to use chevrons for borders.

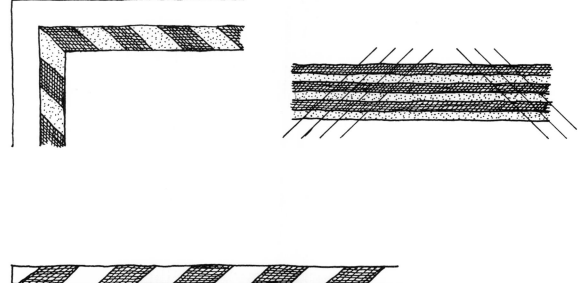

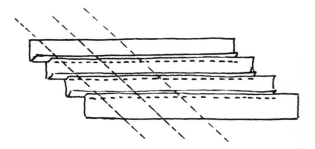

Diagonal Stripe Borders

4-49. How to make borders of diagonal stripes.

A Way to Save Fabric

4-50. A way to save fabric when making wide bands of diagonal stripes.

5

STRIP PATCHWORK WITH WOOLEN FABRICS

The traditional ethnic designs of the world, as found in basketry, ceramics, embroideries, tapestries, rugs, and other textiles, suggest countless ideas for making useful and beautiful things needed in furnishing and decorating the home. Made of woolen fabrics, they simulate the original articles in color, warmth, durability, and richness of surface. Heavy cottons and upholstery fabrics can also be used effectively.

Fabrics about the weight of flannel are excellent to work with. All the materials used in making the examples were easily torn. However, you may find that certain weaves (gabardine, for instance) and some of the blends may need to be cut. Extremely bulky fabrics should be avoided, although you might be able to use plain strips of nubby wool or fleece for textural interest. For blankets and pillows intended for practical everyday use, it is a good idea to prewash the materials in the same way you would wash the finished article. Most of the firmly woven wools suitable to use in the strip technique can be washed in the washing machine in cool water and a mild detergent or soap flakes.

Because woolens are more pliable, as well as thicker, than cottons, it is best the make the seams about one-half inch wide, and to press them open. And it is essential to press thoroughly after each operation, as is done in tailoring. In fact, it is a good idea to think of pressing as blocking the piece; if it is squared up well each time a strip or section is added, problems can be virtually eliminated.

Do not worry if the back of the work looks bumpy and irregular. The seams on the right side will be surprisingly straight and tidy, none the less.

Inspired by the design of a Navajo rug, the blanket shown in Figure 5-1 is made entirely of reused woolens. Pieces were machine-washed in cool water, making this a washable blanket, and all the colors except the light gold are as found in the original garments. White flannel pieces were dyed in the washer to make the gold. The dimensions of the blanket are 66 by 88 inches before finishing the edges. The amounts of fabric given here are based upon using 54-inch-wide woolens: Dark brown, 2½ yards; camel-beige, 1¼ yard; gold-brown, ½ yard; darker greenish blue, ⅓ yard; light grayed-turquoise, ½ yard; cocoa-brown, ¼ yard; off-white, about ³/₈ yard; rust, about 1 yard; gold, about 1 yard; and light rust or orange, about 1 yard.

The long bands across the width of the blanket need to be pieced together. If you are using remnants or discards, piecing will be dictated by the lengths of your materials. If the

fabric is new, use your own discretion about piecing.

Step 1. For the long plain-bands that run across the width of the blanket, make strips as follows:

Color	Quantity	Width
Dark brown	15	2 inches
	3	3 inches
Camel-Beige	15	2¼ inches
Gold-Brown	1	3¼ inches
Gold-Brown	3	4¼ inches
Darker green-blue	3	3¼ inches

Cut three of the dark brown 2-inch strips into 13-inch lengths and add one to each of three 54-inch strips, resulting in three 66-inch lengths (67 inches minus seam allowance). Cut the camel-beige strips to make twelve 66-inch strips; the gold-brown to make two 66-inch plain-bands; and the 3¼-inch strip is 65 inches long. The darker green-blue should make two bands 66 inches for the ends.

Step 2. From the remaining dark brown, rust, gold, and lighter rust, cut strips 4 inches wide. Because I used salvaged wool materials for this project, the lengths of the pieces on hand were mainly about 21 inches. To avoid undue waste of the limited supply of needed colors, the 4-inch strips were sewn together to maximize the number of bias bands that could be cut. See Figure 4–49 at the end of Chapter 4. Don't forget to offset the strips in both directions.

If you are using new material, the same method is recommended. When four strips have been sewn together in the order desired, press the seams open, and join the pieces to one another in the same manner, so that long bias bands 3-inches wide can be cut from them. The colors used in the example are brown, rust, gold, and lighter rust, with some orange interspersed because of a dearth of the light rust color.

5–1. A "Navajo" blanket made entirely of reused woolens. Blanket designed and made by the author.

Step 3. When sewing two of the bias bands together to form the chevron pattern, lay one face up on the board or table, check it for straightness, and pin down if necessary, then lay the other one on top of it, matching the colors and seams (as seen in the example), and lay a yardstick along the seamline, as directed in the instructions for joining diagonal segments. Pin together, and sew.

Note: The arrangement of the chevron bands may be varied as desired; note the example.

There should be six of these bands. Sew the twelve long bands of camel-beige on the sides of them, placing the camel-colored bands on the table face up, with the chevron bands on top. Then add the twelve long bands of dark brown.

Step 4. From 4-inch strips of the grayed-turquoise color, cut twenty pieces 6 inches long, and set them aside. These are to be inserted between the patches with the motifs of white and cocoa-brown. Tear two strips of turquoise 1¾ inches wide, and one each of white and cocoa the same width. Make a strip-band with the white and cocoa-brown strips in the center; press, and cut into eighteen 3-inch segments. Sew these patches between the plain pieces of turquoise to make the two bands shown in the example.

Step 5. Make three strip-bands of white and cocoa-brown with strips 2¼ inches wide to make twenty-four pieces 5 inches long, or 120 inches in all. Cut strips of white about 2½ inches wide to make twenty-six pieces 3½ inches long. Sew the 5-inch pieces from the strip-band to the white inserts, alternately reversing the colors to make the pattern shown at the end of the blanket. Sew the long bands of brown 3 inches wide to one side of each of these bands, and the bands of darker greenish blue to the other sides.

Step 6. The three long bands of gold-brown are sewn between pairs of the chevron bands. If these are not all exactly alike, arrange them as you wish them to be. The turquoise pattern-bands are to be sewn at intervals between the six bands of chevrons. In order to work with smaller sections as long as possible, I found it most convenient to sew the end borders onto the sections with the chevrons and to sew the turquoise bands to each side of the center section. I sewed these three large pieces together last. You will need a large surface to lay the work on and pin it in place before sewing. Remember to press well as you go, with the fabric supported to prevent stretching.

Step 7. To finish the edges face them with bands of wool or other material, and line as desired. The lining could be sewn lightly by hand to a few of the horizontal seams to hold the layers together, if desired.

The group of pillows shown in Figure 5–2 was made of woolen remnants in black, cream, and warm browns, to carry out the African theme of the Peoul blanket on the opposite wall of the room. The fact that there was a limited amount of material to work with resulted in some interesting variations on the original designs. For the pillow of herringbone stripes in Figure 5–3, I made the striped fabric according to the lengths of the pieces I had, cut the diagonal bands in alternating directions, and found I had unequal lengths of these bands. The result is the pillow shown, which measures 14½ inches by 17 inches; one more band of the diagonal stripes would make it square, if desired.

To make it you will need about ⅓ yard of each of two colors, if 54-inch wool is used. If remnants are used you will need the equivalent. Colors in the example are copper and creamy white.

5–2. These pillows in "African" colors were made of salvaged wool and remnants. Pillows designed and made by the author.

5-3. A shortage of fabric contributed to the interesting deviation seen in this pillow of herringbone stripes.

Step 1. Cut or tear five strips of each color $1^7/_8$ inches wide, and sew them together, making a band 54 inches long and about 9¼ inches wide.

Step 2. Press seams, lay them straight on a flat surface, and mark bias segments about 3½ inches wide, as shown in Figure 5-4. It is all right if they vary slightly in width.

Bias Segments

5-4. How to cut a band of stripes made from strips 54 inches long. If you are using shorter remnants, you could end up with an interesting variation all your own.

Step 3. Cut the segments and join them end to end to make two long bands. To make a regular pattern of herringbone stripes, the bands would have to be equal in length. To make the irregular pattern shown in the example one of the bands in the pillow was composed of stripes running in both directions, requiring unequal amounts of the two striped bands. The strip-band described in the directions provides a little extra material.

Step 4. Mark and cut the longer band into three pieces 18 inches long and the shorter one into two 18-inch pieces. Arrange the remaining pieces as desired or as in the example, and sew together, matching the stripes.

A typical Seminole pattern is used to make the pillow shown in Figure 5–5. It consists of one wide strip-band of nine strips in four colors. The patch forming the front of the pillow is 22 by 17 inches when finished. The pillow is made with boxed corners that are formed by stitching across the corners inside. A piece 23 by 18 inches is needed to make the back. The following 30-inch strips are needed:

Color	Quantity	Width
Sandy beige	2	4½ inches
Black	4	2¼ inches
White	2	2⅛ inches
Copper	1	5¼ inches

Step 1. Sew strips together in the following order: beige, black, white, black, copper, black, white, black, beige. Press the seams open. This piece should be about 24 inches long and 18½ inches wide.

5–5. One wide strip-band of nine strips was used in this easy-to-make pillow.

Step 2. Lay this piece face up and straight on a flat surface and mark in from the left on the upper edge 4 inches. Draw a line from the lower left-hand corner to establish the diagonal on which the segments will be cut. Mark and cut ten segments 2⅜ inches wide.

Step 3. Slide the segments down so that the black stripes overlap about ½ inch; mark the edges with pins if desired, before sewing.

Step 4. Press the seams open, and sew the pieces left over to square the corners, matching the stripes according to the example.

The motifs in the pillows shown in Figures 5–6 and 5–8 are formed by matching up the elements in the horizontal bands, rather than by the manipulation of vertical segments. See Figure 5–7. The striped bands are planned so that the colors line up to form various figures.

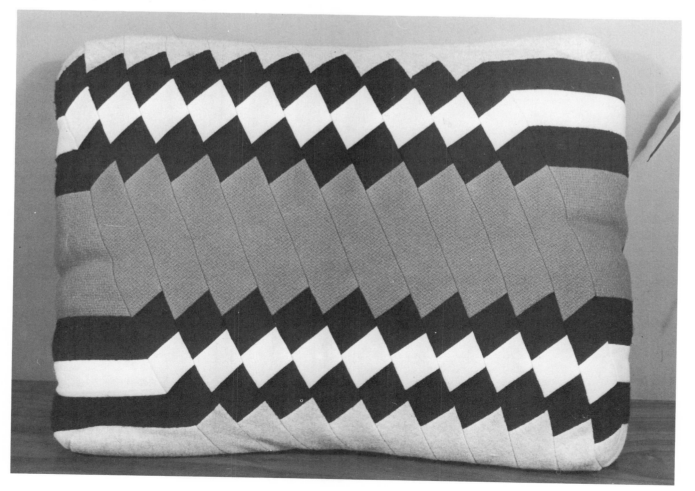

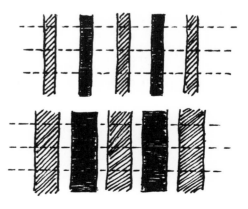

5-6. Narrow horizontal "slices" cut from differing striped bands form the motifs in the top and bottom bands of this pillow. A great variety of geometric figures can be made using this system.

5-7. How to plan a pillow such as the one shown in Figure 5-6.

The finished bands in the pillow shown in Figure 5-6 are about $^7/_8$ inches wide, cut from three different pieces of machine-sewn striped fabric. Colors used in the example are black, white, and camel-color wool. The ½-inch seam allowance is desirable for either wool or cotton to add stability and ease the handling of these narrow-bands. Dimensions of the finished pillow are 16 by 17 inches. Fabric for the back of the pillow is about 18 inches square. To make the pillow you will need the following amounts of fabric: black, 14 by 14 inches for the seven strips between the pattern-bands; black, 18 by 10 inches for strip-bands and pieces on the sides; camel, 18 by 9 inches; and white, 18 by about 10 inches.

Step 1. Make a strip-band 18 inches long, using the following dimensions, and sewing in order:

Color	Width
White	$2^3/_8$ inches
Black	$1^7/_8$ inches
White	$2^3/_8$ inches
Camel	$1^7/_8$ inches

Check the dimensions after sewing and pressing; the black and camel stripes should be $^7/_8$ inches wide, and the white ones $1^3/_8$ inches wide. Cut the band into three pieces 6 inches long, and join them side by side. Press the seams, and cut these bands into three bands about 1¾ to 2 inches wide. Set aside.

Step 2. Make a second strip-band 18 inches long, with colors and widths as given:

Color	Width
White	$1^7/_8$ inches
Black	$2^3/_8$ inches
White	$1^7/_8$ inches
Camel	$2^3/_8$ inches

Cut in three pieces 6 inches long and join as in Step 1. Press seams; cut into bands 1½ inches and 1¾ inches wide.

Step 3. Combine bands from these two strip-bands as shown in the photograph, lining up the colors to make the two patterns shown.

Step 4. To make the row of camel-colored blocks cut a 12½-inch strip of camel-color 3 inches wide and a strip of black 1¾ inches wide. Sew together, press, and cut into 2½-inch lengths. Join them side by side, sew a piece of black to one end, and press.

Step 5. Complete the pillow by sewing plain-bands between the pattern-bands, following the example or arranging as you prefer. Use the 18-inch strips of black at the sides; these can be used to box the corners slightly if you wish.

For the black and beige pillow shown in Figure 5–8 narrow horizontal strips cut from three differing prefabricated striped pieces, as shown in Figure 5–9, were combined to make the rows of motifs. Numerous patterns can be created by using striped bands in this way. Large squares or wide bands of similar figures perhaps somewhat larger in scale would make a handsome cover for a bed or couch.

Approximately ¼ yard each of beige and black wool at least 40 inches wide, are needed for the top of the pillow, and a 16-inch square of either color for the back.

Step 1. To make the row of vertical bars, use 40-inch strips of beige and black, each $1^7/_8$ inches wide. Press, cut, and join three times in the manner shown in Figure 2–11 to make a piece 5 inches by 14 inches, and add a 5-inch strip of black to the camel-colored stripe. Slice this piece in two, making them 2 inches and 3 inches wide. The wider band will be sewn between strips of plain black, and the narrower one will be used for the pattern in the center.

Step 2. Make a strip-band of beige 32 inches long and $3^5/_8$ inches wide, and one of black $1^7/_8$ inches wide. Cut and join twice to make a piece 8 inches long, and add an 8-inch strip of black $1^7/_8$ inches wide to the end. Press seams, and cut into four bands $1^7/_8$ inches wide. Make a second strip-band 24 inches long, with beige $1^7/_8$ inches wide and black $3^5/_8$ inches wide, and cut and join twice to make a piece 6 inches long. Add a 6-inch strip of black $3^5/_8$ inches wide to the end, and cut into three bands 2 inches wide.

Step 3. Combine the narrow-bands of differing colors and widths to make the motifs shown in the photograph. Then sew strips of black between them. These can vary slightly in width from ¾ to 1 inch.

5–8. Another pillow in which the motifs are formed by combining modular strips.

5–9. The three kinds of strips needed to make the pillow shown in Figure 5–8.

5-10. Black ribbons and white triangles alternate as positive and negative shapes in this snappy design, which is easy to make by the strip technique.

5-11. How to cut the striped fabric for the pillow in Figure 5-10.

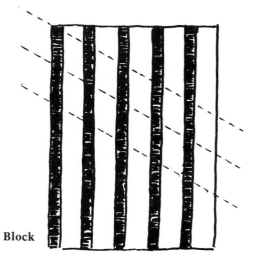

Block

The pillow of white triangles on a black background, shown in Figure 5-10, can also be viewed as white hourglass forms, or as folded black ribbons. The total amount of fabric needed is: white, 24 by 17½ inches; black or charcoal-gray, 24 by about 34 inches; plus an 18-inch square of either color for the back. The patchwork piece for the top is 13½ by 14½ inches when finished, and about 16½ inches square when edged with strips of black.

Step 1. Cut or tear five strips of white 24 by 3½ inches and ten of black 24 by 2¼ inches. Set aside five of the black strips.

Step 2. Make five strip-bands of white and black, taking ½-inch seams. Press seams open and join the bands side by side.

Step 3. Press seams, and lay this piece of striped fabric face up on a flat surface, making sure the seams are straight. Draw a diagonal line from the upper left-hand corner, as shown in Figure 5-11, such that the white points are 60-degree angles to form equilateral triangles. Mark lines at 4-inch intervals, and cut.

Step 4. Sew the remaining black strips between these bands so that the stripes are lined up accurately. You will need to lay a ruler across the seam and mark the edge of each black strip sewn onto a band in order to match to the next striped band. It is important that this step be done carefully.

Step 5. Press the seams and again lay the fabric face up on a flat surface. Lay a yardstick across the centers of the diamonds and draw lines across the fabric. Cut along these lines.

Step 6. The pattern is made by sliding alternate bands to the left and to the right, so that the base of the white triangle is centered over the black strips. Pin the bands together along this edge, checking before sewing to see that the white triangles meet at the corners.

Step 7. Press the piece, and sew strips of black to all four sides to make it about 16½ inches square, or the size desired.

In the wall rug shown in Figure 5-12 strip patchwork is incorporated with machine-sewn patchwork to make a pictorial hanging reminiscent of hand-woven Peruvian textiles. Woolens in natural colors would be most appropriate, although heavy, textured cotton in earthy colors could also be used. The finished hanging is about 25 by 37½ inches.

The yardage requirement given assumes that the fabric has been torn from the bolt (if new), rather than cut. If the end of the fabric has been cut, you cannot be sure that it is cut straight along the grainline of the material, and will need to tear off a strip, or draw a thread to make the end perfectly straight. Be sure to allow for a little extra material for this. Wools about the weight of flannel are pleasant to work with, and can usually be torn easily. Certain weaves and some of the wool-polyester blends may need to be cut. If you plan to use wool from salvaged garments, the strips may be cut either lengthwise or crosswise of the goods, whichever is appropriate, and some of the plain-bands may need to be pieced, but this will not detract from the appearance of the hanging.

Colors used in the example are a yarn-dyed black, medium gray, camel-beige, and off-white. If you plan to use different colors, be sure they include four distinct values from dark to light, distributed as in the example. You will need the following amounts of 54-inch wool: black, ½ yard; gray, ¼ yard; beige, ⅓ yard; and white, ¼ yard.

Before constructing the picture in the center of the rug, it would be best to reserve the fabric needed for the plain horizontal bands and any other long strips required. Make sure the end of the fabric is straight, and trim off the selvages.

Step 1. From the black, cut the following pieces: 18 by 29 inches wide, to be used for making the plain stripes; two strips 4½ inches wide by 22 inches long, and four pieces 4 inches wide by 8 inches long.

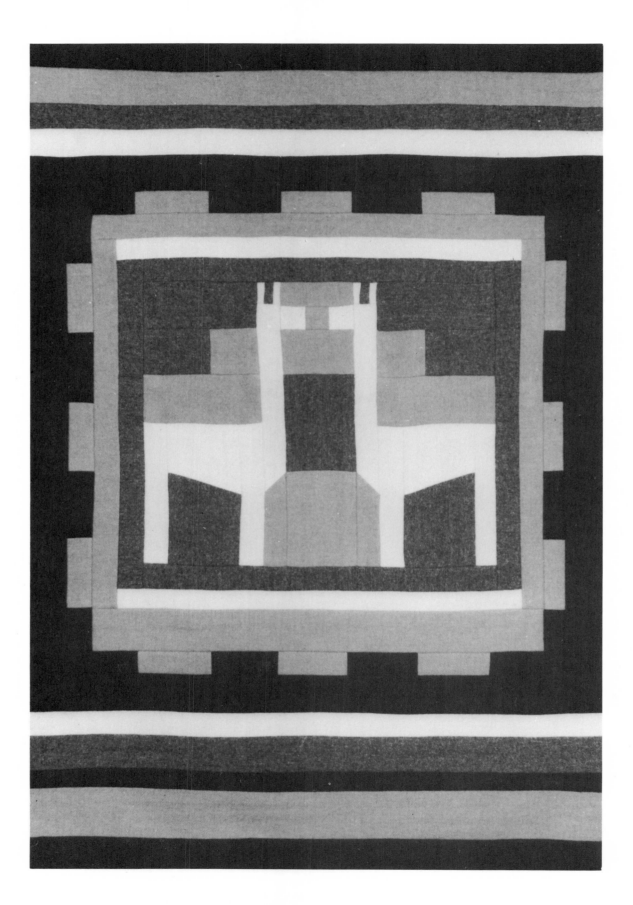

Step 2. From the beige, tear a strip 3 inches wide across the width of the material, and cut into pieces 29 inches and 20 inches long. Tear another piece 2 inches wide, and cut it into two pieces 17 inches long, and one 20 inches long. Pin these three pieces together with the other 20-inch strip of beige, and set aside. You might find it helpful to label this lot "for frame of picture." Also, from the beige, tear a piece 2½ inches wide and 29 inches long, and three pieces 4 by 8 inches. Pin these latter three pieces with the 4- by 8-inch pieces of black to be used for making the striped fabric for the notched border surrounding the picture.

Step 3. From the gray, tear two strips 2 by 31 inches, one 2 by 29 inches, and one 2½ by 29 inches.

Step 4. From the white, tear two strips 2 inches wide across the width of the fabric, and from these cut two pieces 29 inches long and two pieces 18 inches long. Put the 29-inch strips of all four colors together and set aside to use in making the plain stripes above and below the picture.

Step 5. Start to make the picture in the center. For the patches of gray and beige above the body of the llama, make a strip of gray 3 inches wide and 20 inches long. Cut it into two pieces 6 inches long and two pieces 4 inches long. From the beige, make a strip 3 inches wide and 18 inches long, and cut this into two pieces 6 inches long and two 3 inches long. Sew the two shorter pieces together, end to end, as shown in Figure 5–13. Press seams, and add the 6-inch strips of gray and beige to either side of each patch. Press seams and set aside.

Step 6. Make a grid of 1-inch squares, 17 inches wide and 14 inches high, and on it draw Figure 5–13. (The necks and legs of the animals are 1 inch wide.) From this drawing, trace the pattern pieces needed, as shown in Figure 5–14, adding seam allowances.

Step 7. Lay Pattern A on the white fabric and cut two pieces facing in opposite directions. Do the same with Pattern B, and cut four pieces 2 by 7 inches for the legs of the animals.

Step 8. Lay Pattern B on the gray fabric and cut two pieces as in Step 7. Join to the white pieces (see Figure 5–14) and press the seams open. Sew the legs to both sides of each patch, press seams.

Step 9. Sew the above rectangle to the patch made in Step 5, joining the body of the animal to the beige strip.

Step 10. Using Pattern D, cut two pieces of beige, and join them to the neck sections, following the illustration.

Step 11. To make the ears of the animal, use two 2-inch squares of gray. Appliqué or embroider white areas with yarn, either before or after sewing into the piece. Narrow strips of wool were sewn together in the example, but this proved to be awkward.

Step 12. Join the neck patches to the body patches, lining up the seams where necessary, and making sure the two edges are straight. Press these pieces well, making sure the edges are parallel and that the corners are square. They should measure about 7 by 13 inches.

Step 13. For the center portion of the panel, cut a piece of gray 4 by 5 inches, and three pieces of beige, 4 by 2 inches, 4 by 3 inches, and 4 by 5 inches. Join the two 4- by 5-inch pieces across the ends, then add the 4- by 3-inch beige piece to the gray.

5–12. A wall hanging with a llama design is made of woolen fabrics in the neutral shades typical of Peruvian textiles—charcoal, medium gray, camel-beige, and natural-white. Wall hanging designed by the author and made by Adele Byrd.

Step 14. To make the noses of the llamas sew a 2-inch square of beige between two 2-inch squares of white. Press the seams and join this patch to the piece made in Step 13, referring to the illustration. Sew the remaining small piece of beige above the noses, and press the seams. This section should be about 4 by 13 inches.

Step 15. When joining the center section to the sides of the picture, place it face up on the board and lay the side section over it, lining up the seams according to the illustration. Mark, pin, and sew as usual. The piece should now measure about 16 inches in width and 13 inches in height. Press the piece well, making sure the corners are square and the edges are parallel before proceeding.

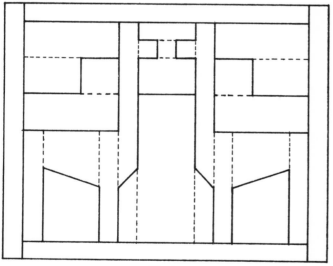

Block

5-13. The pattern for the center of the hanging.

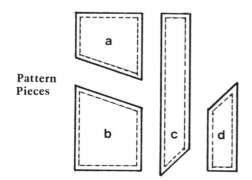

Pattern Pieces

5-14. Pattern pieces for the bodies of the llamas.

Step 16. To sew on the bands surrounding the picture use the two 31-inch-long strips of gray. Cut two pieces 15 inches long, and two 16 inches long. Sew the 16-inch strips to the top and bottom of the picture and the 15-inch strips to the sides. Sew the 18-inch strips of white to the top and bottom. Press well after each addition. Using the four strips reserved in Step 2, sew the 17-inch strips to the sides of the picture and the 20-inch strips to the top and bottom, with the wider one below. When sewing on these strips, place the picture face down over the strip, which should be pinned *straight* on the board. Use a yardstick and a few pins to mark the seamline, as directed in Chapter 1. When this part of the work is finished, check the dimensions to make certain that the bands and the edges are parallel. Make any necessary corrections. Trifling discrepancies in the dimensions can be corrected by a little judicious steaming, stretching, and blocking.

Step 17. To make the striped fabric for the notched border use the four pieces of black and the three pieces of beige 4 by 8 inches. Sew the long sides together, alternating the colors, to make a piece 8 by 22 inches. Mark carefully across the width, and cut into four bands 2 inches wide.

Step 18. Pin one of these bands on the board and match the side of the picture to it, referring to the illustration. The strip should be an inch too long at each end, if the seams in the two pieces are lined up correctly. Place the picture over the strip face down, pin in place, and sew as usual. Trim the extra inch off each end. Repeat for the other side. Join the remaining striped bands to the top and bottom of the picture. After pressing, this piece should be about 22 inches square.

Step 19. Sew the two 22-inch strips of black reserved in Step 1 to the sides of the picture.

Step 20. In sewing on the plain-bands above and below the picture the bands above the design will be sewn on first. Always place the plain-band being joined to the work face up, with the larger piece on top, so that the last seam sewn is visible. This system helps to keep all the seams parallel. Remember to press well after each addition. Be sure each strip lies straight, and be careful not to stretch it. Pin in place along the seamline and mark it if desired. Sew a 2½-inch strip of black to the top of the picture, then a 2-inch strip of white. To this add a 2-inch strip of gray, then the 2½-inch strip of beige. Lastly comes one of the 4½-inch strips of black.

Step 21. In the same manner sew onto the bottom of the picture the 2½-inch strip of black, the 2-inch strip of white, the 2½-inch strip of gray, the 1¾-inch strip of black, the 3-inch strip of beige, and the 4½-inch strip of black.

Step 22. Two inches of material have been allowed around the edges for a smooth, substantial finish. First, baste a 2-inch hem on the two sides of the hanging, and tack it loosely to the back of the work. Press these hems. Turn up the lower hem, clipping excess fabric from the corners as necessary. To make a channel for inserting a rod or stick for hanging the piece turn back a hem at the top, baste, and sew firmly to the seam allowance, leaving the ends open.

If you wish to line this hanging, it would be best to do this after the sides and bottom are hemmed. Cut the lining a little wider than the finished hanging, and a trifle longer. Hem the bottom of the lining by machine and turn back the sides, pressing or basting in place. Place the lining on the back of the hanging, so that it is even with the top of the piece. This will reinforce the channel at the top. Make the hem at the top, then hang the piece and pin the sides in place. Turn the piece to the right side and check to see that the fabric is not drawn up by the lining. It has been my experience that the best way to line fiber pieces that are to be hung is to adjust the lining while the piece is hanging and to leave the lower edge free.

The handsome wall hanging, shown in Figure 5–15, relatively easy to make, was developed from the pattern shown in Figure 4–35. Made of 3-inch strips (2 inches when finished) of dark brown and camel-beige wool, it measures 26 by 40 inches overall and suggests the potential for decorating large wall spaces simply, yet effectively, by the strip-patchwork method.

Oriental carpets are a rich source of interesting motifs and glorious color combinations that can be adapted to the strip technique. Several typical border patterns could be combined to make a large and elegant floor pillow. Kilim rugs, with their many bands of simple geometric patterns and mellow colors, would be most attractive interpreted in strip patchwork for bed covers or as wall hangings. Checking out library materials on ethnic arts and crafts, browsing through import catalogues, or making a tour of import shops should give you a host of ideas for ways to use the strip technique to make useful articles of enduring beauty and real worth.

5-15. A large-scale wall hanging of brown and beige wool. The motif in the center is made by combining the blocks shown in Figure 4-36. Designed by the author and made by Lassie Wittman.

STRIP PATCHWORK FOR CLOTHING

Strip-sewn patchwork can be used in clothing to fulfill various purposes. It makes a good substitute for expensive woven or embroidered braid trimming and can be made in various widths to fit individual requirements. Decorative elements, such as collars, cuffs, neck bands, pockets, yokes, vestees, belts, and borders, can be designed especially to fit an original creation, or can be used to individualize ready-made garments; and, of course, bands can be inserted to make things larger or longer.

Materials used in a strip-band to be inserted in the garment should be of similar weight and character. However, patchwork made of lightweight material may be applied to clothing made of somewhat heavier fabrics. The idea of using silks or silklike synthetics, is appealing, but, because of their tendency to slip out of place, experiments to date seem to indicate that working with such materials may be too exacting and time-consuming to be practical. Heavier fabrics that are firm and smooth, such as kettle cloth, sail cloth, and lightweight denim, work well in sturdy articles where bold, uncomplicated patterns are most appropriate.

Patchwork trim on clothing need not be complicated in order to be effective. The shirt shown in Figure 6–1, made of natural-colored heavy cotton crash, is quick and easy to make.

Bands of chevron stripes, made as shown in Figure 4–48, are applied over the shoulder seams and down the sleeves, which are faced with bands of striped print cotton in black and gold.

6–1. Easy-to-do strip patchwork enhances a natural-colored cotton crash shirt. Shirt designed and made by the author.

6-2. The simple patchwork bands used to trim this navy blue tunic work well both vertically and horizontally. Tunic by Lassie Wittman.

6-3. Patchwork in bright pastels was used on this colorful jacket of coral-colored Calcutta cloth. Jacket made by Joanne Haldeman.

To make the checkered fabric for the front trim, sew together four strips, each 33 inches long and 1¾ inches wide, in the following order: dark print, light color # 1, dark print, light color # 2. Press and cut this band into three pieces, each 11 inches long. Sew these striped pieces side by side to make a piece of fabric 11 inches long by about 15 inches wide. Press again, and cut across the stripes to make 6 bands 1¾ inches wide each. Arrange them as shown in the photograph and sew them together, leaving open the upper portion of the center seam. Trim the upper end to fit the neckline of the shirt. Stay-stitch the outer edges, clipping or ripping the inside corners as needed, and press back the edges ¼ inch.

With the right side placed against the inside of the shirt, sew it to the neck opening. Bring the piece to the outside, press it flat, and pin it carefully in place, taking care not to stretch it. Use thread in the dark color to stitch it down, and to stitch the slotted hem and embellish the lower edges of the sleeves.

For the simple navy blue tunic shown in Figure 6-2 a pattern was chosen for the vestee and deep borders on the sleeves that works well vertically, as well as horizontally.

Pattern-bands in bright pastels are pleasingly combined with coral-colored calcutta cloth in the colorful and practical jacket shown in Figure 6-3. Plain narrow bands were sewn to the pattern-bands, which facilitated applying them to the body of the jacket. The pattern-bands were attached to the jacket before the shoulder seams were joined. Applying the bands, rather than inserting them stripfashion, eliminated the need to line the jacket. Yet, this made a jacket heavy enough to be comfortable in cool weather. (The Seminoles, of course, do not line their skirts or the men's shirts.) However, to eliminate extra bulk in the sleeves the patchwork for them was done in the Seminole manner and then cut out. The entire jacket could be made in this way, if you prefer, and lined. Rickrack braid was added to accentuate the typical Seminole design.

The attractive and very wearable shirts, shown in Figures 6-4 and 6-5, which are both made of Calcutta cloth, illustrate the fact that bold, simple designs that are relatively easy to make can be very handsome. While not all pattern-bands work well when used vertically, the front panel on the shirt in Figure 6-4 is especially successful and not complicated to make. The designer has commented, however, that care is needed in matching the stripes at the center front, where the zipper is sewn in. By using wider plain-bands close to the front opening, this problem was eliminated in the shirt shown in Figure 6-5.

Well-designed and expertly tailored, the elegant ski outfit shown in Figure 6-6 has fine braidlike patchwork on the collar, sleeves, and front of the jacket, and encircling the knees of the pants. Beneath the outer shell of white poplin, waterproof nylon encloses the layer of Dacron insulation.

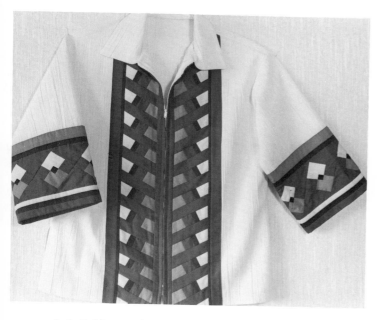

6-4. Bold, simple patterns are effective on this shirt-jacket of cream-colored Calcutta cloth. The dark-colored bands used to edge the sleeves and form the panel down the front are practical, too, for hiding soil. Shirt by Pat Albiston.

6-6. Finely made strip patchwork in light blue, red, navy, and white makes the rich, braidlike trim on this elegant ski outfit. Outfit designed and made by Rosemary King.

6-5. Another shirt-jacket, with the light color used at the edge of the patchwork band silhouetting the row of points on the front panel. Shirt by Pat Albiston.

Bands of diagonal stripes in subtle colors are used to enliven a green cotton vest, shown in Figure 6–7. This would be a relatively simple way to use bands of strip patchwork with your own basic pattern. Here the bands are inserted into the back to form a yoke, with a knotted tie and stuffed tassels added.

In a striking departure from the traditional Seminole way of using diagonal square patches, the designer of the square dance dress shown in Figure 6–8 simply enlarged the scale of the pattern and eliminated the addition of plain edging strips to create a stunning effect. The elaborate patch is composed of seven different segments, and is similar in principle to that shown in Figure 4–25. The squares in the skirt were sewn together, as shown in Figure 2–17, but with strips of plain color interspersed to separate them. Those on the sleeves were applied. The dress is of bright, orangey coral, with the motifs in black, white, apricot, and orange shades. The orange in the patches disappears into the background, emphasizing the black and white pattern.

Figure 6–9 is a detail view of a long hostess apron. This is a clever way to handle a flared bottom border. To make the bands that trim the outer edges of the apron, a single wide pattern-band was made and cut in half down the center, saving considerable time and effort.

6–7. Bands of diagonal stripes inserted between bands of plain light green cotton make the front of this attractive vest and form a yoke in back. Vest designed and made by Phyllis Bradfield.

6–8. Enlarged Seminole patches are used without bordering strips to make a striking square-dance dress. Dress designed and made by Lassie Wittman.

6–9. The lower edge of this long hostess apron shows an interesting solution for fitting a straight band to a flared edge. The pattern-band of chevrons, used across the front, is joined to those on either side with a plain-colored segment in a wedge shape. Another way to fit segments to a curved edge is to taper them by taking each seam in a little deeper at one end when joining them. Apron designed and made by Kay Kelly.

6-10. Fabrics with patterned stripes add distinctive touches to a child's dress of red print cotton and greatly enhance the simple design of the strip patchwork inset. Dress by Phyllis Bradfield.

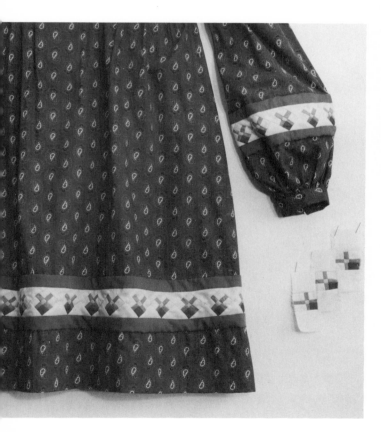

6-11. This popular Seminole pattern looks charming edged with strips of blue and inserted at the hemline and into the sleeves of a simple dress of red cotton with small blue paisley figures. Dress made by Joanne Haldeman.

The body of the apron is of a rich shade of rust, with patchwork of blue-greens, rust, and white. The patchwork on the pockets is repeated across the top of the bib. Other ways to make a curved band are to taper the segments to fit the desired curve or simply to take the seams slightly deeper at one end of the segments as you join them.

Strip patchwork is used here very effectively to decorate the vestee in the child's dress shown in Figure 6-10. The fabric is a red cotton print. Colors and values, as well as the patterns, are well chosen and show that the patchwork elements need not be elaborate to produce an excellent design.

The charming dress shown in Figure 6-11 is of red cotton with a small paisley motif. The pattern of red and fresh spring green on white, banded with blue, looks like a row of strawberries and is most appealing. Figure 6-12 shows the segments needed to make the motif and a similar patch often seen in Seminole bands. Figure 2-17 shows how to sew these patches together to make a band of diagonal squares.

The patch shown in Figure 6-13 appears more elaborate than the ones in Figure 6-13, but, actually only two different segments are used to make the pattern.

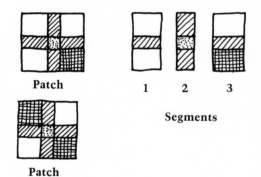

6-12. Three different segments are needed to make the patch for the band in Figure 6-11.

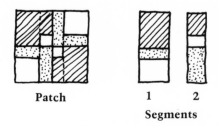

6-13. A similar patch, although it appears to be more elaborate than the one in Figure 6-12, requires only two segments.

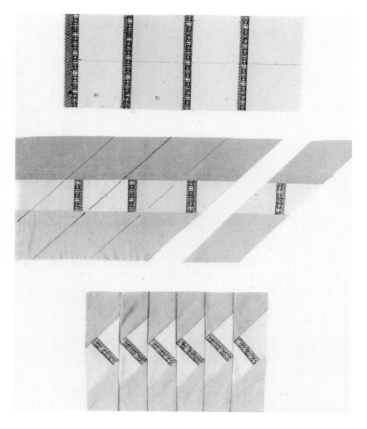

6-16. A contemporary Seminole band and how to make it.

6-14. The pattern in the skirt of this child's dress is essentially the same as that seen in Figure 6-11, but appears different because of the scale and placement of the patches. Narrow figured strips enrich the simple patchwork, which is shaped at the neckline by wedge-shaped insertions. Dress designed and made by Phyllis Bradfield.

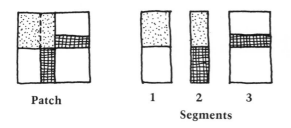

Patch   1   2   3
                            Segments

6-15. Segments needed to make the patch in Figure 6-14.

The smart little dress in apricot, orange, and black striped prints shown in Figure 6-14 has a motif in the skirt which is very similar to the one shown in Figure 6-12, but the effect is quite different. To make the sawtooth band fit the round neckline, extra wedges of plain fabric were inserted between the segments. This could be avoided by making the neckline square, although the curved neckline is a pleasing variation from the straight horizontal bands. Figure 6-15 shows the segments needed to make the pattern.

The pattern shown in Figure 6-16 is often seen in contemporary Seminole designs and is done as follows:

1. The strips are sewn together, cut crosswise, and sewn end to end to make a long band.
2. Bands of plain colors are sewn to each side.
3. The resulting band is cut into diagonal segments and marked for matching.
4. Segments are sewn together, with the edges trimmed.

Patchwork elements were inserted into the ready-made T-shirts shown in Figure 6–17. In the dark shirt the armhole seam was ripped out in front, and the area to be replaced with the patchwork band was reinforced with light-weight pellon before being cut. Figure 6–18 shows how to insert patchwork into a garment by machine.

Step 1. Cut the pellon exactly the same size and shape as the patch to be inserted, and pin carefully in place on the right side of the garment. (Baste if desired.)

Step 2. Stitch the pellon ¼ inch from the edge. Mark a dotted line ¼ inch inside the line of stitching. *Before* cutting, press the seam allowance in toward the center of the patch.

Step 3. Cut along the dotted line, and clip carefully through both fabrics on the inside curve and into the corners.

Step 4. (The reverse side of the fabric is shown, with the pellon turned in and pressed flat.) Pin the patch along the seam so that the edges match the edges of the pellon piece. Stitch along the previous line of stitching. (The half-circle of pellon represents the patchwork piece being inserted.)

6–17. Blocks or bands of strip patchwork can be inserted into ready-made T-shirts for a touch of individuality. T-shirt designs by Lassie Wittman.

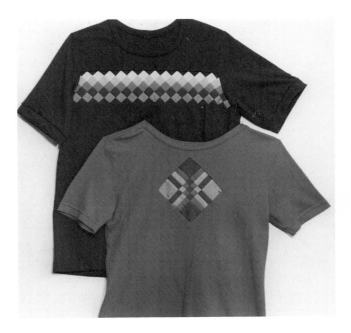

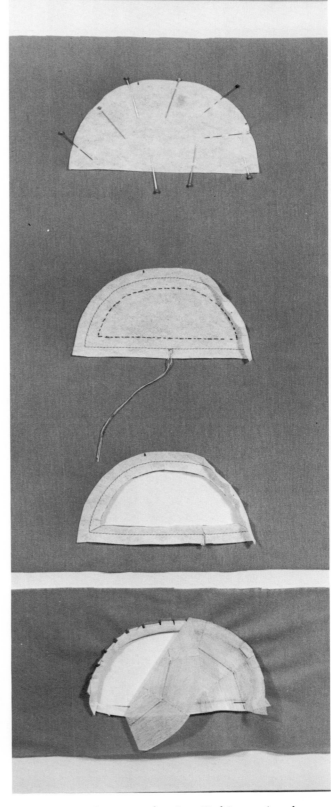

6–18. How to insert patches into T-shirts, using the sewing machine.

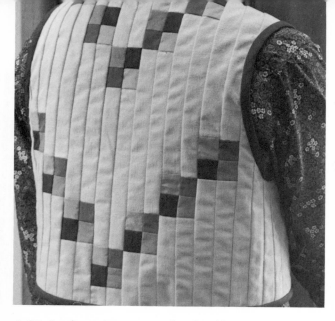

6-20. As the strips go over the shoulders, the pattern of small patchwork blocks changes.

6-21. The side view shows how the design works. Bolero designed and made by Donna Prichard.

6-19. This brief bolero, made entirely of 1-inch strips of fabric, has a quilted effect.

The clever bolero shown in Figure 6–19 appears to be cut from a single "piece" of strip-sewn fabric, with blocks of patchwork set into it. Notice in Figure 6–22 how the patchwork strips actually change as they go over the shoulder. Long segments 1 inch wide give the effect of a quilted surface. The patchwork is done in green, warm yellow, orange, and melon, on oyster-white kettle cloth. The designer recommends that a muslin be made and corrected to fit the wearer, but made slightly larger than required, in order to allow for the take-up of material by the seaming. Add at least an inch for length. Aside from the fact that it would be difficult to alter the finished garment without spoiling the effect, she found it helpful to use the muslin pattern as a guide as she proceeded. See Figures 6–20 and 6–21 for the back and side views.

The strip-bands made for the front were 11 inches wide. Be sure the segments for both sides of the vest are in the correct order before cutting them. Four strip bands 24 inches long were needed, two of each color combination, as shown in Figure 6–22.

6-22. Drawing showing the basic plan of the bolero. This idea can be adapted to make a variety of vest designs or to make a front inset all-in-one with a back yoke for a shirt or caftan.

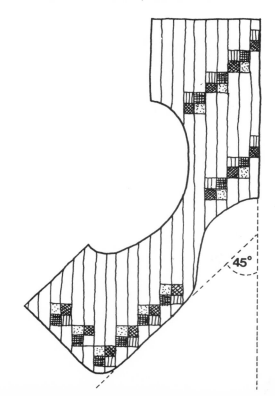

45°

This idea could be varied, with the front section going over the shoulder to form a yoke across the back, with perhaps a contrasting color used for the back and sides to match a skirt or pants. In this small vest the front edge makes a 45-degree angle with the line continued up from the center back, as shown in Figure 6–22. If your pattern requires a different angle, the pattern-band would be designed accordingly. Draw lines indicating the segments needed on a full-scale paper pattern, and use this to plan the patchwork pattern and the dimensions of the strips needed.

A wide band of sewn strips cut into gores and alternately reversed makes a graceful patchwork skirt that eliminates fullness at the waist and adds it at the bottom. The skirt shown in Figure 6–23, which is 34 inches long from the lower edge of the waistband to the hem and 86 inches around the bottom, was cut from fabrics 42 inches wide.

The total amount of fabric needed is about 3 yards. See Figure 6–24. From 1¼ yards of Color A, four strips 10 inches wide are cut or torn, and the remainder used for the waistband. Of the four other colors, two strips 6 inches wide of each color are needed. If purchasing fabric especially for this skirt, allow a little extra to make sure the edges of the strips are on the grain of the fabric. To make the skirt the desired length hem the lower edge and trim the excess from the top.

This patchwork looks best if the value contrast is minimized; contrast is achieved through the juxtaposition of warm and cool colors within a limited range of dark and light tones. (Colors used in the example are blue, beige, turquoise, and brown.) An assortment of pastel colors would be charming; or deep-toned velveteens, brocades, and taffetas would make this a handsome skirt for holiday wear to be worn with a blouse of the same color as the top and bottom bands. Shown in Figure 6–25 is an alternative plan for a floor-length skirt to be made from 45-inch fabrics. Strips of Color A are 13 inches wide, and the others are seven inches wide.

6–25. A variation of the plan in Figure 6–24 for making a long skirt.

6–23. A quick and easy patchwork skirt, cut to flare gently at the lower edge. Skirt designed and made by the author.

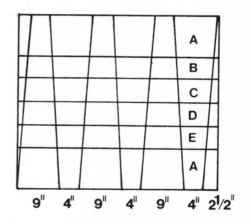

6–24. How to make the bands for the skirt in Figure 6–23.

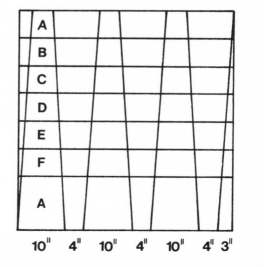

101

7

STRIP PATCHWORK IN BOUTIQUE SEWING

For making small articles, such as bags, pillows, pincushions, toys, tree ornaments, and other gifts, the strip patchwork technique is ideal. One 45-inch strip-band provides enough segments for several items. Segments from various bands can be interchanged and combined in different ways so that no two articles are identical, and waste of work and material can be eliminated by combining scraps and leftovers in small articles, such as pincushions, small bags, or eyeglass cases.

Small waist aprons trimmed with a single band and pocket of patchwork are easy to make and suitable for sale at fund-raising bazaars. For a group project, the work might be divided between those who make the pattern-bands and those who sew the aprons. Other possibilities for bazaar projects are place mats, table runners, pot holders and mitts, tea cosies, and neckties. Patchwork elements such as pockets, yokes, and bands of trimming might be packaged to be applied on or inserted into the customer's own garment.

The bag of natural-colored linen shown in Figure 7–1, with the patchwork in warm yellow, rust, and black, was made by the author, using narrow-bands cut from four different prefabricated pieces of black and yellow stripes. For the gift shop artisan, these bands could be combined differently in each article, so that each bag would be truly one of a kind. Figure 7–2 shows how the end of the bag was cut and how it is sewn in so that it folds inward when closed.

The bags with flaps shown in Figure 7–3 are made of suede fabric and of black wool and make effective use of a minimum of patchwork. The bag on the right is made up of elements cut from two strip-bands. It would be practical to make this bag in quantities. The pattern for this is the same as the one in the quilt shown in Chapter 4, Figure 4–7.

Corduroy in beige, bronze, and dark brown makes the sturdy tote bag shown in Figure 7–4. The pattern of 3-inch blocks is simple and well suited to its purpose.

Figure 7–5 shows a bag that makes good use of printed fabric and a pleasing arrangement of plain-bands to augment the band of patchwork. Here again, a single pattern-band is used effectively.

Figure 7–6 shows an excellent project for bazaar sales or Christmas gifts. The segments for the band in this gingham apron are 2¾ inches wide, (2¼ inches when sewn), and the borders for both the bib and the lower edge can be made from one 45-inch strip-band. The bib measures 10 inches across, and the lower edge 34 inches. Colors in the patchwork are white, apricot, warm light green, and bright yellow calico print, on yellow-and-white checked gingham.

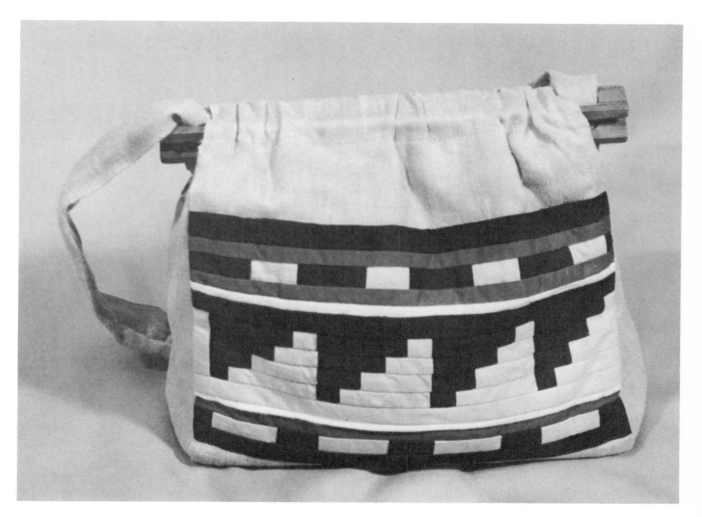

7-1. Narrow horizontal strips form the pattern in this bag of natural-colored linen, with trim of black, spice brown, warm yellow, and a touch of white. The basic system for making patterns in this manner is shown in Figures 5-7 and 5-9. Bag by the author.

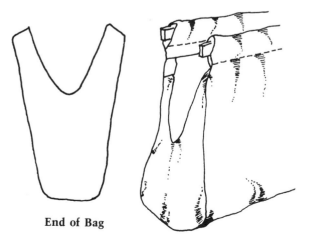

End of Bag

7-2. Pattern for the end of the bag in Figure 7-1.

7-3. Strip patchwork trims the flaps on two bags, one of wool and the other of suede fabric. The patchwork pattern used in the bag on the right is shown in Figure 4-9. All bags made by Lassie Wittman.

7-4. A simple, large-scale pattern is appropriately used on this sturdy tote bag of beige, bronze, and brown corduroy. Bag by Liz McCord.

7-5. Although it includes only one simple pattern-band, this bag is effective because of the way the printed fabric and the bands of dark and light are used. Bag by Rosemary King.

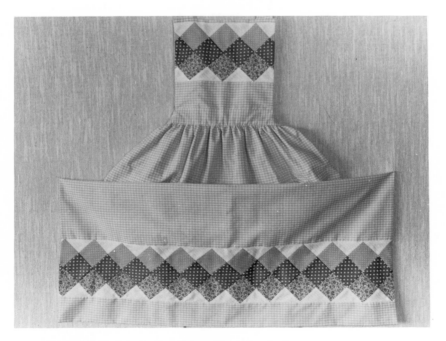

7-6. The patchwork trim for this yellow checked gingham apron can all be made from one 45-inch strip-band. Apron designed and made by Liz McCord.

7-7. Calcutta cloth in soft blues, coral, and white make the crisp design in the center pillow, made by Lassie Wittman. The other two pillows were made of bands and patches left over from larger projects, by Joanne Haldeman, and demonstrate the logic and convenience of the strip technique for making a variety of gifts.

See Figure 7-7. Pieces leftover from the jacket shown in Figure 6-3 made the colorful pillow on the right. Bands left over from the quilt in Figure 4-25 were used to make the one on the left. The pillow in the center is of Calcutta cloth in soft medium blue with white and rosy rust tones.

In the pillow shown in Figure 7-8 the pattern-bands were placed on the diagonal. Plain narrow bands are pleasingly arranged between the pattern-bands and enhance the distribution of the dark and light values.

The pillows shown in Figure 7-9 are easy to make and surprisingly effective. The middle one combines black and gold velveteens, rust-colored corduroy, printed corduroy, and woven braids that give the appearance of wool. The pillow on the right contains squares, diagonally cut from one strip-band. The way the values are distributed in the strip-band creates a very attractive pattern.

The good-looking pillows shown in Figure 7-10 were made in rich deep tones of wine, rust, gold, and black in corduroy and velveteen.

The delightful pillow shown in Figure 7-11 is of bright yellow with bright rose and black, and combines tassels of pearl cotton with strip patchwork to make the charming baubles for the corners.

Strip patchwork helps to shape these animals, shown in Figure 7-12. Strip patchwork could be similarly employed to embellish stuffed toys made from purchased patterns, using cotton prints in rich deep tones of reds, blues, browns, black, and gold.

Clean, crisp blues and white with a touch of red make the attractive set of place mats shown in Figure 7-13.

7-8. Typical Seminole patterns look fine when placed on the diagonal, as they were in this pillow. Made by Kay Kelly.

7-9. The simple pattern in the cotton pillow at the left is repeated in the one in the center, which is of deep-toned velveteen, corduroy, and machine-woven woollike braid. Diagonally striped squares cut from strip-bands of four colors make the pleasing pattern in the cotton pillow at the right. All pillows made by Liz McCord.

7-10. Two large handsome pillows of velveteen and corduroy in dark, rich colors use bold, simple patterns appropriate to their size. Both pillows designed and made by Pat Albiston.

7-11. The small patchwork squares and tassels at the corners of this delightful pillow greatly enhance the simple band of three motifs. Designed and made by Pat Albiston.

7-12. Bands of strip patchwork are incorporated in the designs of these cleverly made stuffed animals. Animals designed and made by Phyllis Bradfield.

7-13. Crisp patterns in navy, red, light blue, and white are combined with plain-bands of the same colors to make an elegant set of place mats. Mats made by Rosemary King.

7–14. Small purchased boxes with short lengths of pattern-bands set into the tops make useful and attractive gifts. Boxes by Pat Albiston.

Small-scale patchwork is set into the tops of the wooden boxes shown in Figure 7–14. Available in craft and hobby shops, the boxes can be painted or finished as desired.

A simple checkered band makes a fitting design for a necktie of light brown sports-weight cotton, as shown in Figure 7–15. Since neckties are cut on the bias, it is not difficult to insert the pattern-band along the straight grain of the fabric. Colors are beige, blue, light gold, brown, and deep orange with a narrow plain-band of orange above and brown below.

Figure 7–16 shows tiny pillows in red, bright greens, and white exquisitely made to trim a Christmas tree. The stuffed blocks and the dolls were made by the author. Bands of three strips, such as what would be made for the Nine Patch quilt block (see Chapter 4), were used to make the blocks, and were sewn together by machine. The dolls are made from a band of five strips, and the pattern is reversed on the band to make optimum use of the strip-band. To stuff the dolls rip the seam at the waistline on one side, rather than leaving a portion of the outer seam unsewn. The figure can then be stuffed from the center into both ends, and the seam is easy to close by hand.

7-15. Colorful but not gaudy, this summer necktie of light brown heavy cotton has a band of patchwork in soft yellow, orange, blue, and brown set into it along the straight grain of the fabric, making it a relatively simple project. Necktie by the author.

7-16. A variety of Christmas tree ornaments made with sewn strips. The stuffed blocks are made of segments such as those that would be used to make a Nine Patch quilt block, two such segments being sewn together by machine to form a cube, with an opening left for stuffing it. The dolls were cut out like a row of gingerbread men, from bands of five strips that make the hats, faces, shirts, pants, and boots of the figures. When sewing together the two sides of the dolls, sew completely around the outline, and rip the seam at the waist to turn and stuff it. Not only is it easier to stuff the ends from the middle of the body, but it is easier to sew up the opening. The tiny pillows, exquisitely made, are by Lassie Wittman.

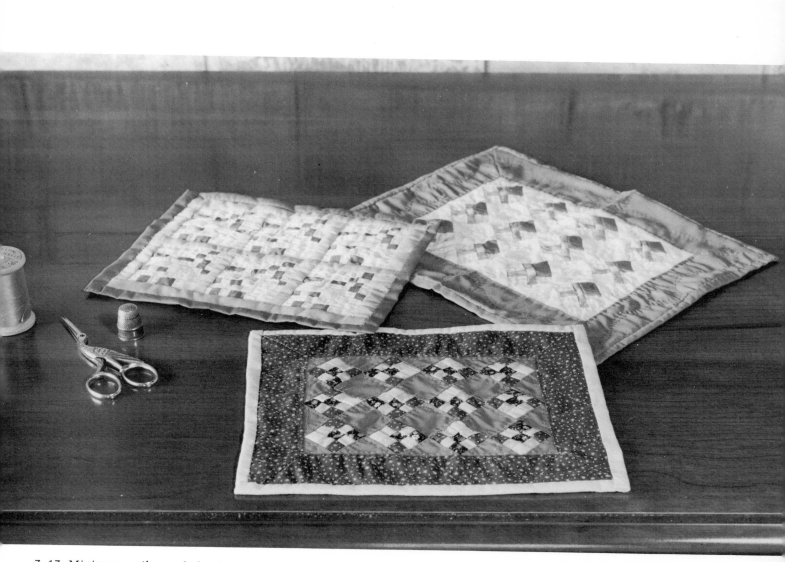

7-17. Miniature quilts made by the strip technique. The quilt in the foreground has a Nine Patch pattern. On the left is one with a rosebud pattern similar to a needlepoint design. The one on the right has a tiny Seminole patch. All made by Joanne Haldeman.

Miniature quilts, shown in Figure 7-17, are made with ¼-inch segments. In the foreground in the photograph is a tiny version of a Nine Patch quilt. The pattern in the quilt at the left is similar to a rosebud done in needlepoint, although the colors used do not convey the motif clearly in the photograph. Because a number of differing segments are required to make patterns of this kind, it would be most practical to make several small articles at a time. These patterns could also be used to simulate embroidery for trim on clothing.

The pictorial patch shown in Figure 7-18 was designed to be applied to a dark blue denim tote bag. Colors in the body of the cat are light blue and soft medium blue print, with yellow for the eyes and a bit of red for the nose. It could also be used to make a quilt for a child, with lighter color for the background and lattice bands in a contrasting color to separate the blocks.

Directions are given for making the standing cat. The diagram for making a sitting cat is also shown, for which the dimensions of the strip-bands would need to be altered.

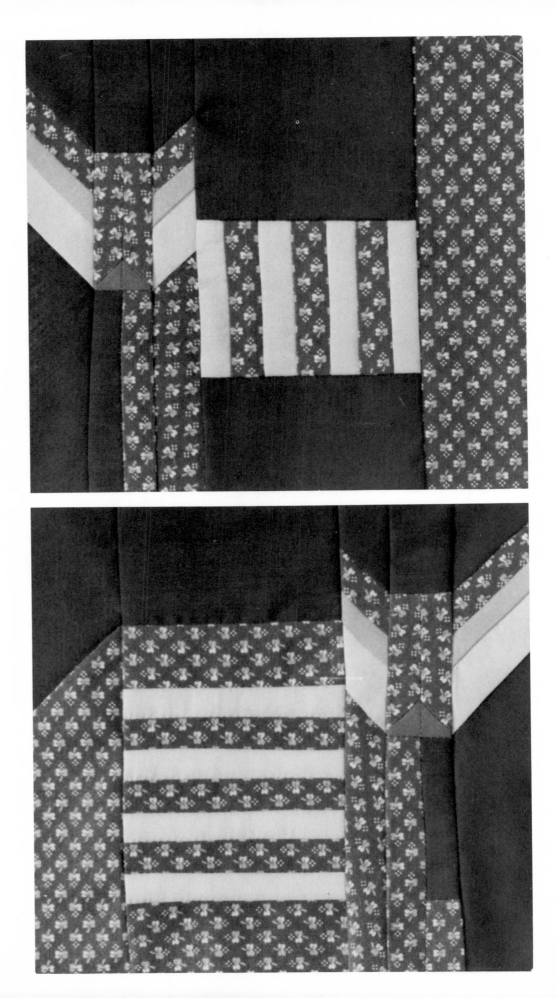

For this kind of patchwork it is necessary to make patterns for the segments required, to facilitate the matching of the parts.

Use graph paper to enlarge the patterns for the segments shown in Figure 7–19 to the desired dimensions, and make patterns of tagboard or transparent plastic film, showing the lines denoting the colors in the strip-bands; making the patterns on heavy transparent film would be a great convenience. On Pattern # 3, draw the diagonal line on both sides.

The following amounts of fabric are enough for segments for eight of these patches. Making fewer is relatively impractical, since the design is intended especially for making bags or pillows for gift shops or bazaar sales: dark blue cotton, ⅓ yard; blue print (medium value) ⅓ yard; plain light blue, about 6 inches; plain red, 1 by 28 inches; and bright yellow, ⅞ by 44 inches.

Step 1. Make a strip-band 44 inches long, using strips of the following colors sewn together in the following order:

Color	Width
Light Blue	1¼ inches
Yellow	⅞ inch
Blue Print	1 inch
Dark Blue	2½ inches

Press seams toward the dark blue, and cut in two pieces, 21 and 23 inches long. To the light blue strip on the 23-inch band sew a strip of dark blue 4 by 23 inches, and to the 21-inch band sew a strip of the blue print 4 by 21 inches. Using Pattern # 1 on the 23-inch band, mark and cut eight segments. Use Pattern # 2 to make eight segments from the 21-inch band.

Step 2. Make a strip-band 28 inches long of the strip of plain red and a strip of the blue print 2½ inches wide. Press this seam *open*. Using pattern # 3, cut eight segments for the left side of the cat's face, and reverse the pattern to cut eight more for the right side.

Step 3. Make a strip of dark blue 8 inches long and 3⅝ inches wide, and one of the blue print of the same dimensions. Sew the small patches for the left side of the face carefully to the strip of dark blue, along the end with the red triangle. Then sew the remaining patches to the strip of blue print. Cut apart into 1-inch segments. Compare with Pattern # 4 to make sure they are straight, and correct if necessary.

Step 4. Taking one segment for each side of the face, match the center seams and sew together, following the illustration. Tear a strip of dark blue 12 inches long and 2¾ inches wide. Press and sew these patches to it, along the end with the blue print. Cut apart into 1½-inch segments.

Step 5. Matching seams where necessary, sew segments made with Pattern # 1 to the left side of these patches, and segments made with Pattern # 2 to the right side.

Step 6. To make striped fabric for the body of the cat tear strips 24 inches long, four of the light blue and three of the blue print, all 1 inch wide. Sew together, alternating the colors. Press the seams and cut into eight 3-inch pieces.

Step 7. For the areas above and below the body of the cat, you will need about 54 inches of the dark blue material, 4 inches wide. From this, cut eight pieces 3¾ by 4 inches and eight 2½ by 4 inches. Sew one of each to the ends of the striped patches. After pressing, join these pieces to those that form the front part of the figure, according to the illustration.

Step 8. From the blue print, cut eight strips 8¼ by 2 inches to complete the figure. One-half inch has been allowed for turning back the edges of the patch.

See Figure 7–20 and if you want to make the sitting cat.

7–18. These patches with cat figures, one standing and one sitting, could be made to decorate tote bags or pillows, or to make a quilt for a child. Several of the patches can be made from the segments cut from one of each of the required strip-bands, making them convenient to make in quantity. Designed by the author. Patches made by Mathia Walesby to test the author's directions.

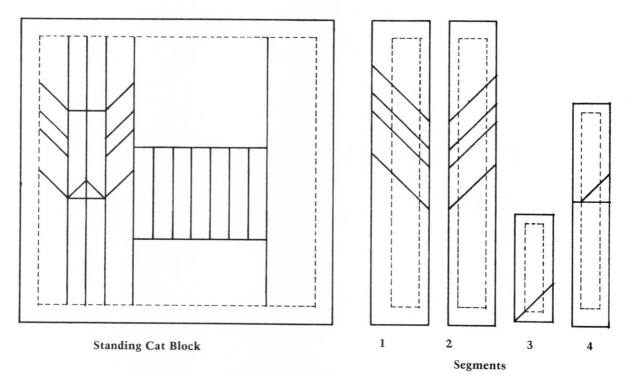

Standing Cat Block　　　　1　　2　　3　　4

Segments

7-19. The pattern for the standing cat figure and the segments needed for making it.

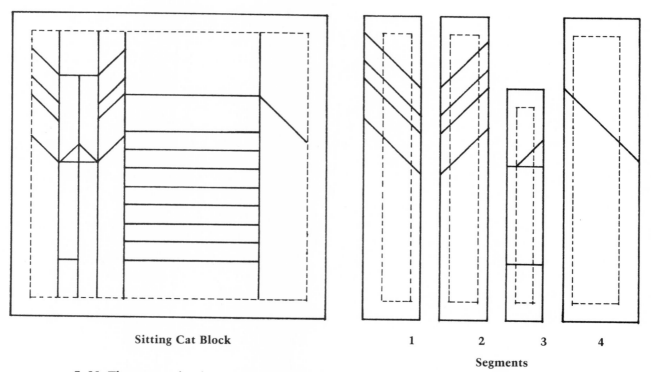

Sitting Cat Block　　　　1　　2　　3　　4

Segments

7-20. The pattern for the sitting cat figure and the segments needed for making it.

STRIP PATCHWORK FOR A CHRISTMAS BANNER

In the Christmas Tree banner shown in Figure 8–1 the colors are two shades of avocado green, light warm reds, and some strips of blues and gold. Other colors could be used. The list of fabric requirements given here indicates the value scale used in the original as a guide for your color planning.

For the narrow-bands at the top and bottom of the banner, I used a printed striped fabric in deep bright blue and one narrow strip of gold print that were both found in my scrap box. These touches of unrelated color add life and sparkle. Ribbon, braid, or metallic rickrack could also be used.

It is recommended that swatches of the colors you select be mounted on a card and numbered to correspond with the colors on the list; this should facilitate following the directions as given. The following amounts of fabrics are needed for the pattern-bands: lightest value: Light avocado green (Color # 1), ⅝ yard; middle values: plain warm red (Color # 2), ⅙ yard, Red calico print (Color # 3), ⅙ yard, Soft blue-and-green print (Color # 4), 1 by 20 inches; darkest values: Plain avocado green (Color # 5), ¾ yard, avocado print (Color # 6), 3 by 45 inches, darker avocado print (Color # 7), 1½ by 45 inches.

The hanging shown is of dark natural-colored linen, but any color could be used, depending on the colors selected for the pattern-bands. For the panel, you need a piece about 25 inches wide and 30 inches long. For the lining, you need a light, firm fabric, such as si bonne, 30 inches long; ½ yard of lightweight pellon and a ⅜-inch dowel 22 inches long are also needed.

Step 1. To make a pattern for the tree shape fold and cut a large sheet of paper to make a triangle 18 inches high, 17 inches at the base. Draw horizontal lines parallel to the base line, 4¼ inches, 9¼ inches, and 13 inches above the base line. These will serve as guide lines when joining the pattern-bands.

Step 2. From the pellon, cut a similar triangle 17½ by 16½ inches, to make the foundation for the tree form. Also make a small cardboard pattern to use as a guide in cutting segments, by drawing two legs of the angle at the lower corner of the tree shape and drawing lines parallel to them, making a diamond with sides about 3 inches long. Cut a 2½-inch square of pellon to be covered with fabric for the trunk of the tree. Make a pattern for the base of the tree, to be cut of the pellon, according to the dimensions given in Figure 8–2.

8-1. An appealing holiday banner mingles a lively array
of pattern-bands in warm tones of red, and dark and
light avocado greens. Christmas tree hanging designed
and made by the author.

116

Step 3. To make Pattern-Band 1 (bias stripes, bottom band) tear a 45-inch strip of Color # 2 1 inch wide and join to the 1½-inch strip of Color # 7. Make a piece of striped fabric by sewing these strips together, cutting in half, and joining the pieces side by side twice (in the manner shown in Figure 2–11. The resulting patch should be 11 inches long and 6½ inches wide.

Step 4. Place the pattern on the fabric, folded as shown in Figure 8–3, and mark across the top to establish the cutting line. Remove the pattern and extend the line across the fabric, using a ruler. Measure down from this line 2⅛ inches and up 2⅛ inches, and draw lines for cutting. If the fabric is difficult when folded, unfold the material and mark the lines on each side, making sure to reverse the direction of the diagonal lines. Join the shorter pieces to the longer pieces, end to end, and join these to make a V at the center.

Step 5. To make Pattern-Band 2 (poinsettia) you have to combine segments from two different strip-bands, plus inserts of plain color. Make the strip-bands 10 inches long.

Strip-Band	Color	Width
Strip-Band A	Color # 5	2½ inches
	Color # 5	2½ inches
	Color # 5	⅞ inch
	Color # 2	⅞ inch
Strip-Band B	Color # 5	3 inches
	Color # 5	3 inches
	Color # 2	⅞ inch

For the insertions, use a strip 6 inches wide and about 25 inches long, cut into twenty-eight vertical segments ⅞ inches wide. After sewing and pressing the bands and cutting them into ⅞-inch segments, assemble the flower motifs by sewing one segment from Band B between two segments from Band A, matching the corners of the red squares. Sew insertions on as shown in Figure 8–4.

Press the five flower patches, lay them right side up, and mark the edges with pins as shown in Figure 8–5. The spaces between the dotted lines should be about ⅜ inch.

Step 6. Sew a segment from Band B to each side of one of the flower patches, matching the corners of the red squares with pins, and set it aside to be used for the band near the top of the tree. Join the remaining patches so that there are three small red squares between the four flowers. Add three or four plain segments to each side of the single-flower patch, stepping them down to form a band of bias segments. In the same manner, add six or seven plain segments to each side of the longer band. The shorter band should be about 7 inches long and 3⅜ inches wide. The longer one, about 17 inches, should be trimmed to 3 inches in width. Be sure to trim the edges parallel to the center of the band.

Alternative ways of combining these segments, which eliminate the necessity of marking the edges of the segments for matching, are shown at the end of the chapter in Figures 8–9 and 8–10.

Step 7. To make Pattern-Band 3 (diamonds) make a strip-band 22½ inches long, using two strips of Color # 1, 1¾ inches wide, and 1 strip of Color # 5, 1¼ inches wide. After sewing and pressing, lay the pattern on the band as shown in Figure 8–6 and draw a line along one side to establish the cutting line. Mark and cut 1¼-inch segments.

Slide the segments up from left to right to form the row of diamonds shown. Join the segments, matching corner to corner. Press, and trim the edges to make a band about 2½ inches wide.

Step 8. To make Pattern-Band 4 (checkered band) make a strip-band 24 inches long, with strips of the following widths:

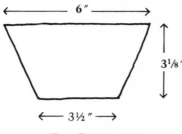

Tree Base

8-2. Pattern for the base of the tree.

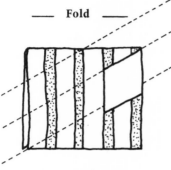

Fold

Cutting Lines

8-3. Making the bottom band.

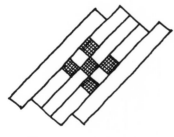

Motif

8-4. "Poinsettia" motif in Band # 2.

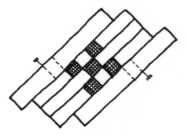

Mark Edges With Pins

8-5. How to mark the edges of the patches for matching to the single squares.

Color	Width
Color # 1	1¾ inches
Color # 6	1 inch
Color # 2	1⅛ inches
Color # 5	2 inches

Cut the band in vertical segments ⅞ inches wide, and join by sliding alternate segments up, so the red corners touch, forming a checkered pattern. Trim to 3¾ inches wide.

Step 9. To make Pattern-Band 5 (red and green points) make a strip-band 18 inches long, of Color # 3, 2 inches wide, and Color # 5, 1¾ inches wide. After sewing, press the seam toward Color # 3, and place the band on the board with this color at the bottom. Lay the pattern on the band to establish the angle of cutting the diagonal segments, mark at 1⅜-inch intervals, and cut the segments. With Color # 3 at the bottom, mark the segments on the right-hand edge ⅞ inches below the seam, as shown in Figure 8-7.

Match the seam of one segment to the pin on the next, press, and trim to 2¼ inches wide.

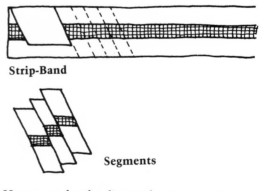

Strip-Band

Segments

8-6. How to make the diamond pattern in Band # 3.

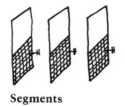

Segments

8-7. How to mark the segments when making the row of points in Band # 5.

Step 10. To make Pattern-Band 4 (small diamonds) tear strips 20 inches long as follows:

Color	Width
Color # 1	1½ inches
Color # 4	1 inch
Color # 2	1 inch
Color # 5	1¼ inches

Sew together in the order given, press the seams toward Color # 1. Using the pattern as shown previously, mark a diagonal on the band, mark and cut segments ⅞ inches wide. Slide the segments up from left to right as in previous diamond pattern, matching the corners of the small red diamonds. Trim the band to about 2¼ inches wide.

Step 11. Now you are ready to join the pattern-bands. To prepare the narrow-bands which join the pattern-bands, refer to Figure for guidance. The arrangement of light and dark values is vital to the design. Experiment with the colors of the narrow-bands before putting the pattern-bands together. These bands vary in width from ¼ to ½ inch when finished.

Use the large paper pattern as an aid to check the placement of the pattern-bands. The first line above the base line marks the top of the lower poinsettia band; the checkered band lies between the next two lines; the top line marks the bottom of the single poinsettia motif. So do not worry if your measurements do not correspond exactly to the example. If you find that one of the bands is wider than desired, simply sew a deeper seam, unless it happens to run across the tips of a row of points.

When joining sections, keep the narrow-band on top so that you can see its finished width. As you proceed, check occasionally to see that the bands are parallel; and don't forget to center the bottom band and the two poinsettia bands.

Seam allowances on the pattern-bands are about ½ inch. Allow scant ½-inch seams on the narrow-bands, and use a ruler to mark the seamline with pins, as directed previously, to keep the seams straight.

Since joining the pattern-bands is the most demanding aspect of this project, other alternatives are suggested for the less experienced seamstress. The bands could be basted to pellon to form with the edges touching, and ribbon, braid, lace, or rickrack sewn over them; or folded bands of bias fabric could be used.

When all the pattern-bands are joined, check the measurement and make adjustments if necessary before sewing on the patch for the top of the tree. For this, use a scrap of red calico print, perhaps one different from that used in the pattern-band, about 5 by 2½ inches. Sew narrow strips of Colors # 1, # 5, and # 3 to one side of this piece, and join it to the band with the poinsettia.

In the example, narrow strips of red are used below the band of green diamonds and above the band of red and green points.

Step 12. You are ready to finish the tree shape. Lay the completed patchwork wrong side up and press it lightly on the back, allowing the seams to lie as inclined. You may need to trim some of them. Place the pellon foundation on top of the patchwork piece, making sure the centers of the two are lined up and that the bottom of the pellon is placed so that the narrow-band at the bottom of the tree will be about ¼ inch wide when folded back. Trim the uneven edges of the patchwork about an inch or so larger than the foundation. Pin together here and there, and press the raw edges back over the foundation. Pin, baste, and tack in place so that the stitches do not show on top. Tack lightly to the seaming of two or three bands to hold the layers together.

Step 13. To make the fabric for the base of the tree make a 24-inch strip-band of

Color # 3, 1⅜ inches wide and of # 5, ¾ inch wide. Fold, and cut in half. Join the pieces side by side, cut the resulting band into three pieces 4 inches long, and again side by side to make a piece of striped fabric. Sew a strip of Color # 1, 7 inches long and ¾ inch wide across the stripes, and add a strip of Color # 5 so that the lighter color is a scant ¼ inch wide.

Cover the tub shape cut from pellon with this striped patch, folding and pressing so that the darker band is about ⅝ inch wide and five of the narrow stripes are centered on the pattern. Tack the edges in place. For the trunk of the tree, cover the square of pellon with a piece of Color # 5, folded over the two sides.

Step 14. Your next step is to make the trim at the bottom of the banner. The points that trim the bottom edge are made of hexagons folded and stitched on the raw edge. Two sizes are needed, one with sides 3¼ inches and one with

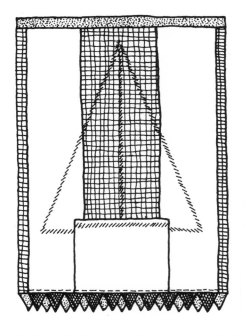

8-8. The back of the hanging, showing how the lining is made to support the bottom trim and prevent sagging of the panel.

sides 2⅛ inches. Make a pattern of each size, and cut ten of the larger hexagons from Color # 5 and eleven of the smaller ones from Color # 1. Fold each one in half, then in thirds. Press, and stitch along raw edge. On a 24-inch strip of fabric or tape (any color), mark 1 inch from each end and also at 2-inch intervals, making eleven spaces. Pin this strip to the ironing board, taking care not to stretch it. Pin the triangles of Color # 1 to this strip between the marks, using a straightedge to keep the bottom edge of the points in line. Then stitch in place. Sew the darker triangles between them so that they hang about ¼ inch below the others.

Step 15. To start putting it all together trim the fabric for the background 24 inches wide and 29 inches long. Make sure the fabric is cut along the grain and that the selvage is trimmed. Baste a line down the center. Use three colors for the narrow-bands at the bottom. The colors in the example are gold, deep blue, and red. Sew these together as desired, and press the seams away from the strip to be sewn to the panel. Join to the panel, then press the seams in the opposite direction and sew to the row of points, allowing ½ inch for the seam. Place this band carefully so that stitching line runs across the line where the triangles meet.

Because of the weight of the bottom trim and the patchwork, it is helpful to use the lining fabric to support these forms and correct any sagging that might occur. Cut two strips of lining material about 7 inches wide and 30 inches long. Across one end of these, press a 1-inch hem, and sew these pieces to the sides of the banner so that the raw edge at the bottom of the strip will be turned under when the lining is folded back. Be careful to have the lining easy enough to prevent the edge from drawing up, but not so full as to ripple. Taking care with lining and finishing are important in making hangings; many good pieces of work are marred by lack of attention to this detail. (See Figure 8-8.)

Step 16. Fold back the lining and press the sides of the panel so that it is 22 inches wide, or as wide as the bottom trim. Pin the lower edge of the lining to the trim and baste it in place. Baste to the top of the panel also.

To make the trim for the top and a casing for the dowel sew together three strips of the colors desired, each 24 inches long. The lightest color, which makes the casing, is 2¼ inches wide; other strips could be ¾ inch and 1 inch wide. Press the seams toward the wider strip, and fold the ends in to make this band 22 inches long, or the width of the panel. Sew to the top of the panel. Fold the band to make a casing for a ⅜-inch dowel. Pin it firmly in place, and stitch through all the thicknesses along the seam between the two top strips.

Step 17. Next comes sewing the tree form to the panel. Place the tree form on the center of the panel, about 2¾ inches from the top and 7¼ inches from the bottom. Pin it in place, and baste around the edges. This may be easier to do from the back. Before sewing it in place, hang the banner to see if it hangs nicely, and to see that the fabric is not drawn up or sagging in places. If necessary, correct by ripping

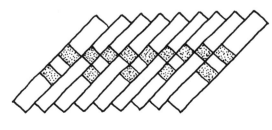

Segments

8-9. An alternative and simpler way to arrange the segments in Band # 2.

the tree from the panel as needed, and repinning it while the panel is suspended. (The lining can also be manipulated to correct problems.)

Slip the square of fabric for the tree trunk up under the lower edge and pin it in place. Then lay the tub shape over this so that the trunk is about 1⅝ inches long. Baste in place, hang again, and check before sewing. Sew the tree form onto the panel from the back, taking loose diagonal stitches around the edges, and make a row of stitches down the center to anchor it firmly in place.

The example was finished by adding a piece of the lining material to the lower edge of the banner, long enough to tack to the lower edge of the tree form and support the bottom trim. The same thing could be accomplished by using a piece of fabric the full length of the panel.

There are alternative ways to mount and finish the banner. The border of folded points at the bottom of the hanging is very attractive and adds an elegant finishing touch to the design. However, the piece could be finished in several other ways. It could be sewn onto sturdy fabric stretched over a frame. In this case it would be advisable to stretch the fabric on the frame *before* pinning the tree in place, then removing the fabric from the frame to be sewn, in order that both pieces are stretched the same amount. Even simpler would be to wrap the tree form over a cardboard foundation and glue it to a board covered with fabric. Narrow-bands of color could wrap the edges, or perhaps a simple pattern-band could be added as trim.

There are also alternative patterns for poinsettia bands and here are some:

1. Instead of insertions of plain fabric, make a strip-band using Color # 5 with a ⅞-inch strip of Color # 6 sewn to the center. This would eliminate the necessity of marking the edges of the segments with pins for matching.
2. Segments from the two strip-bands could be sewn in the pattern shown in Figure 8-9.
3. Segments from Strip-Band # 1 only could be arranged as shown in Figure 8-10. Longer strip-bands would be needed, to provide more segments.

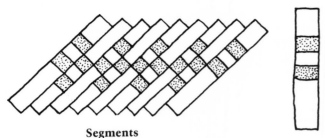

Segments

8-10. Another alternative to Band # 2, which requires only one strip-band.

Similar hangings, with simplified pattern-bands could be designed and made by a group to be sold at fund raisers. The pattern-bands could be made by various individuals in their own homes. If they were all made 45 inches wide, they could be sewn together with the intervening strips to make a large piece of fabric, and this could then be cut to make four tall triangles 18 inches at the base, by reversing the tree pattern on it. It would probably be best to have it mounted on a board or a frame, as suggested above.

Other, more complicated designs could also be made by a group for sale at a bazaar. The next three banners, although not exclusively done in strip patchwork, were all entirely machine-sewn.

In Figure 8–11 hand-dyed linens were used to make a large hanging, which was beautifully sewn by machine and enriched with hand-quilting. The piece measures 36 by 62 inches and combines raw silk, cotton, rayon, and linens in deep maroon, off-white, warm gold, purple, and dusty pinks. As you can see, elements of Seminole patchwork were incorporated into the design.

Seen in color, the wall quilt in Figure 8–12 is a delight to behold, with its lovely rich reds and blue-greens interspersed with areas of cool pastels. Fortunately, the organization of the dark and light areas makes the design almost equally satisfying in black and white. The design combines typical Seminole patterns with an interesting variety of patchwork elements.

The piece shown in Figure 8–13 was inspired by the colors and patterns in a Seminole man's tunic of the 1890s. In the original, the body of the shirt is of a lovely cool green, with pattern-bands of black, cream, and shades of red and rust, with plain narrow-bands arranged to create rhythmical spaces. Some blues and grayed greens were added here in the intervals between the pattern bands. Because of the fine disposition of colors and spaces in this long panel, which is 21 inches wide by 6 feet long, the eye is carried up and down within the composition in a lively and exciting way.

It has only been in the past few years that people have begun to appreciate the sewing machine as an art tool. The three banners shown here demonstrate the enormous potential for the creation of significant decorative works through sewing machine techniques. Fabric art has a warmth and richness of texture that is a welcome contrast to walls of wood, brick, and concrete, and can rival fine paintings, murals, and tapestries in color and design. It is hoped that through strip patchwork, as well as other techniques in fabric, you will learn to discover the fabric arts.

8-11. Carol Tate uses hand-dyed natural fibers and hand quilting to enchance her elegant machine-sewn fabric murals. This one also incorporates Seminole patchwork.

8-13. This wall hanging was inspired by the typical tunic of a nineteenth-century Seminole man. Banner by Kay Kelly (see color section).

8-12. Various patchwork elements were combined with strip patchwork to make this impressive wall quilt by Phyllis Bradfield (see color section).

BIBLIOGRAPHY

Arizona Department of Transportation. *Arizona Highways Magazine* Vol. L1, No. 5 (May, 1975): 32.

Art Institute of Chicago. *"The Native American Heritage."* Catalog for exhibit, July 16–October 30, 1977.

Capron, Lewis. "Florida's 'Wild' Indians, the Seminoles." *National Geographic* 110 (December, 1956): 819–40.

———. "Florida's Emerging Seminoles." *National Geographic* 136 (November, 1969): 716–34.

———. A brief history of the Seminoles prepared for the Historical Society of Fort Lauderdale, Inc., 840 NE 12th Ave., Fort Lauderdale, Florida 33304.

Davis, Hilda. "The History of Seminole Clothing and its Multi-Colored Designs." *American Anthropologist* 57 (October, 1955): 974–80.

Davis, Hugh J. Jr. "Sewing Art of the Seminoles." *McCall's Annual* 6(1955):61–3.

Feder, Norman. "Seminole Patchwork." 6 (September–October, 1959):1–18.

Foreman, Grant. *Indian Removal.* Norman, Oklahoma: University of Oklahoma Press, 1969.

Garoutte, Sally, "Seminole Patchwork." *The Quilter's Newsletter Magazine* Vol. 5, no. 8 (August, 1974):10–11.

Hutchinson, James. "Painting Among the Seminoles." *American Artist* April, 1966:53.

Kiva, Lloyd. "The Crafts of the Indian." *House Beautiful* Vol. 113 (June, 1971):37–39, 132–136.

McCauley, Clay. "The Seminole Indians of Florida." *Annual Report of the Bureau of Ethonology, Fifth Annual Report* 5:477–531, 1883–4.

McReynolds, Edwin C. *The Seminoles.* Norman, Oklahoma: University of Oklahoma Press, 1957.

United States Department of the Interior, Indian Arts and Crafts Board. "Seminole and Miccosukee Crafts." *Smoke Signals.* 47–48 (Winter–Spring, 1966):5–8.

Whiteford, Andrew Hunter. *North American Indian Arts.* Racine, Wisconsin: York: Golden Press, 1979.

Zarbaugh, Mrs. Scott. "Seminole Patchwork." *The Quilter's Newsletter Magazine* Vol. 5, no. 10 (October, 1974):11–12.

Two immensely interesting works on the history of the sewing machine are:

Lewton, Frederick Lewis. *The Servant in the House.* Smithsonian Annual Report, 1929.

Rogers, Grace Cooper. *The Invention of the Sewing Machine.* Smithsonian Institution, U. S. Government Printing Office, 1968.
Three excellent basic books on quilt patterns and quilt making are:

Hinson, Dolores A. *Quilting Manual:* New York: Hearthside Press, 1970.

Ickis, Marguerite. *Standard Book of Quilt Making and Collecting.* New York: Dover Publications, 1949.

McKim, Ruby Short. *One Hundred and One Patchwork Patterns.* New York: Dover Publications, 1962.

The following two books are valuable for inspiration and ideas and show colored photographs of entire quilts. No patterns or instructions are given.

Holstein, Jonathan. *Pieced Quilt: An American Design Tradition.* Greenwich, Conn: New York Graphic Society, 1975.

Safford, Carleton L., and Bishop, Robert. *America's Quilts and Coverlets As Design: A Survey of American Bedcovers.* New York: E.P. Dutton, 1972.

METRIC CONVERSION CHART

LINEAR MEASURE

1 inch = 1,000 millimeters = 2.54 centimeters

12 inches = 1 foot = 0.3048 meter

3 feet = 1 yard = 0.9144 meter

SQUARE MEASURE

1 square inch = 6.452 square centimeters

144 square inches = 1 square foot = 929.03 square
  centimeters

9 square feet = 1 square yard = 0.8361 square meter

INDEX